INDIA

THE W🌏RLD VEGETARIAN

Roopa Gulati

INDIA
THE WORLD
VEGETARIAN

BLOOMSBURY ABSOLUTE
LONDON • OXFORD • NEW YORK • NEW DELHI • SYDNEY

For Dan and our Friday night suppers.

INTRODUCTION

Regional Indian cooking is unrivalled for its breadth of flavours, textures and diversity.

Whether meals are enjoyed on silver thalis, banana leaves or palm leaf plates, what we eat provides us with a blueprint of belonging and identity.

The country's varied landscapes include the fertile plains of Punjab in north India, where crisp ghee-laden layered parathas, tarka dal and simple cumin-spiced vegetables are staples. Then there's the arid, desert-like climate of Rajasthan, where nature has been less kind. But its seemingly meagre resources are compensated for by culinary creativity, and many classic dishes are slow-cooked in yoghurt to conserve scarce water supplies.

Contrast this with south India's palm-fringed coastline and verdant spice gardens. An everyday masala in Kerala might feature mangoes or pineapple, folded into simmering coconut milk, spiked with the crackle of curry leaves, popped mustard seeds and sizzling red chillies. It's all change across the north east, where dishes are cooked in pungent mustard oil and often spiced with the region's signature blend of panch phoran. This heady mix of whole fennel, fenugreek, cumin, nigella and mustard seeds, is dropped into hot oil, where it releases a sweet-astringent pickled flavour, such as in Bengali chutney.

Around 70 per cent of Gujaratis are vegetarian and savoury dishes, including dals, are marked by sweet jaggery and tart tamarind as key flavours. There are at least 60 types of lentils and pulses used across India and it's easy to be overwhelmed by the variety. But dals are forgiving and open to interpretation – most home cooks don't even bother with a specific recipe. For a country shaped by dietary preferences and regional likings, the sheer range of dishes based on the humble lentil commands nothing but respect. There's usually a pot of daily dal on the go in most kitchens, but lentils and pulses are also a valuable base for fried snacks, such as pakoras, savoury doughnuts and crepe-like pancakes. A little leftover dal can even be kneaded into chapati dough to enrich and add texture and an earthy flavour to the bread, before it is cooked on a griddle.

Some vegetarian communities, such as the Jains, don't eat onion or garlic, as they believe that these ingredients heat the blood and promote impure thoughts. They follow the philosophy that digging up vegetables from the ground could injure insects and other living creatures, and their tenet is to do no harm to life. Strictly speaking, orthodox Jains won't even eat root vegetables or tubers, so potatoes would be swapped for plantains and even turmeric would be off-limits. Jains are famed for their imaginative recipes and have honed a vibrant cooking style, which incorporates such spices as umami-like asafoetida and tangy mango powder, bringing big flavours to everyday vegetables.

Dairy produce plays a central role in the Indian vegetarian kitchen. Milk-based dishes are offered to the deities in temples across north and central India, and also have auspicious connotations at celebrations. Dishes cooked in 'pure ghee' are also seen as an indicator of wealth and indulgence.

Sharing culinary know-how is a largely oral tradition with huge regional variations on how best to cook family favourites. Definitive recipes are few and spice blends vary across the country and even within families. Traditionally, a mother-in-law passed prized recipes to her daughter-in-law rather than her own daughter, because, after marriage, the daughter would be cooking a new set of heirloom recipes belonging to her husband's family. Even today, the kitchen continues to be a source of influence, especially in large extended families where recipes are retained and respectfully valued.

Chillies are integral to Indian cooking; today, India is the largest producer of chillies in the world but it's worth noting that it was the Portuguese who brought them from the Americas to India in the 16th century. The Portuguese also introduced garlic, tomatoes and potatoes from the New World to Goa on the western coast. Today, there are dishes, which have been adopted and then adapted from the Portuguese, such as the famed vindaloo with its garlicky-vinegary masala and abundance of dried red chillies.

The Mughals introduced India to Persian dishes in the 16th century and left behind a lasting culinary legacy, which combined Middle Eastern flavours with local Indian produce. Although they were best known for extravagant kebabs and meaty curries, there remains a small but carefully curated collection of vegetarian dishes, which often gets overshadowed. Their distinctive style of cooking embraced masalas made with pounded nuts, which were scented with complex aromatic spices. This two-way exchange of ideas found favour with vegetarian Hindus, who developed a taste for rich culinary indulgence and incorporated such spices in their own cooking. In addition to the Persian and Portuguese influences in shaping the country's cooking, Britain, France, the Netherlands and Southeast Asia have had greater or lesser roles in the evolution of its culinary history.

In return, India's greatest export has to be its cooking. From curry houses on the high street, to pop-up cafés and fine dining establishments – there's barely a country on this planet that doesn't fly the flag for all things masala.

Although a few Western vegetarian dishes still feature on colonial-style menus in India, they tend to favour the likes of baked vegetables cloaked in béchamel sauce, where the wildest spice used is a pinch of white pepper. Historically, Indian cooks triumphed in enlivening colonial offerings, by adding raunchy garlic, ginger and chillies to roasts, toasted spices in soups and even pounded chillies over potato chips. It's these dishes that have been cherished over the years. Chilli cheese toast is one such legacy, which is as likely to be found on a club bar menu as in a home kitchen.

Despite the recent popularity of international fast food chains in India, traditional street stalls continue to draw in the crowds. Some snacks are a mix of hot and cold items, such as warm potato cakes, surrounded by yoghurt and topped with herby chutney. Others, such as bhel puri and fruit chaat are served at room temperature and major on tart-tangy flavours. Chickpeas and potatoes are especially obliging for carrying sauces, roasted spices and creamy yoghurt.

Perhaps no other snack encapsulates India's heritage than the samosa. Samosas are said to have originated in the Middle East and early references can be traced back to the 10th and 11th centuries, when they were described as 'sambuskan'. These snacks were easy to carry on long journeys and were popularised by Arab merchants travelling to India on the old Silk Route. They were also probably brought over by maritime traders. Meat-filled samosas were a feature of Mughal banquets, but after the introduction of potatoes by the Portuguese in the 16th century, vegetarian Hindus quickly adapted these for fillings and made them their own. The list of samosa fillings is limited only by our imagination, but a good starting point is the classic potato and pea filling favoured by hawkers in the bazaars of the old quarters of Indian cities.

This recipe collection travels around India and provides inspiration for armchair cooks, kitchen novices and practiced hands. Recipes have been gleaned from mothers and grandmothers who measure ingredients by handfuls and rarely consult their handwritten notebooks, but consistently turn out fabulous family feasts. There's also input from maharajas in opulent palaces, chefs in upmarket restaurants and street hawkers selling their food in remote villages in the Himalayas. Wherever you live, this is a book that will transport you to India without ever having to leave the comfort of your own kitchen.

SMALL PLATES

CHANNA CHAAT
CHICKPEA SALAD

This snack (*chaat*) is a salad of lemon-drenched chickpeas, mixed with diced red onions, tomatoes and potatoes. It's showered with ruby-red pomegranate seeds and seasoned with chaat masala (see page 52), which features mango powder and nutty-tasting toasted cumin as its star players.

Although I'm a fan of cooking chickpeas from scratch, this recipe does stand up well using the canned variety – just remember to rinse the brine off them before using. This is a simple salad to assemble and its big bold character makes it great choice for entertaining a crowd.

SERVES 4

1 x 400g can of chickpeas,
   drained and rinsed
1 red onion, finely diced
2 tomatoes, deseeded and diced
175g new potatoes, boiled until
   tender and diced
juice of 2 lemons
2 green chillies, deseeded
   and finely chopped
2 teaspoons ground roasted
   cumin seeds
¼ teaspoon Kashmiri
   chilli powder
2 teaspoons chaat masala
   (see page 52)
3 tablespoons chopped
   coriander
3 tablespoons
   pomegranate seeds
½ quantity date and tamarind
   sauce (see page 167)

FOR THE MINT YOGHURT
125g full-fat Greek yoghurt
½ teaspoon caster sugar
2 tablespoons chopped
   mint leaves
1 small garlic clove, crushed
salt, if needed

Mix the chickpeas with the red onion, tomatoes and potatoes. Add the lemon juice, chopped chillies, ground cumin, chilli powder and chaat masala. Gently fold everything together and leave to one side for 10 minutes to allow the flavours to mingle.

Meanwhile, make the mint yoghurt. Combine the yoghurt, sugar, mint and garlic and taste for seasoning, adding a little salt if necessary. Set aside until you're ready to serve.

When you're ready to serve the chaat, add the chopped coriander and pomegranate seeds, then spoon over the mint yoghurt and drizzle with the date and tamarind sauce.

BABY SPINACH PAKORAS

Pakoras are deep-fried snacks that are usually made from vegetables dunked in spiced gram-flour batter and served piping hot with tangy chutney. Regional variations abound, and favoured ingredients include cauliflower florets, onion rings and sliced potatoes in northern India; aubergine roundels, leafy vegetables and eye-wateringly hot green chillies in Gujarat and Rajasthan; and mashed, spiced potato in Mumbai. In West Bengal, pounded lentils add texture to pakoras and in southern India, crackling curry leaves add a local flavour.

This recipe blends gram flour with rice flour, which gives it an extra crunch. A tangle of fried baby spinach leaves will look great on the plate, but you could use ripped-up large spinach leaves – just remember to remove the tough central stem first. Rainbow chard or kale could also work well.

SERVES 4

Sift the gram flour, rice flour, salt, turmeric and chilli powder into a mixing bowl and stir in enough cold water (about 200ml) to make a smooth batter with the consistency of thick pancake batter.

Heat the oil in a karahi or wok over a medium heat. The oil is ready for frying when it reaches 180°C on a food thermometer, or when a cube of bread dropped into the oil browns in 30 seconds. Wash the spinach and pat the leaves dry with kitchen paper, then coat them in the batter. Drop them into the oil, one at a time, and deep-fry in small batches for about 30 seconds each, until crisp and golden. (Alternatively, deep-fry in a large, wide, sturdy pan no more than two-thirds full with oil.)

Drain on kitchen paper and sprinkle generously with chaat masala. Serve with the Bengali tomato chutney on the side.

150g gram flour
75g fine rice flour
1½ teaspoons salt
1½ teaspoons ground turmeric
1½ teaspoons Kashmiri chilli powder
500ml sunflower oil, for deep-frying
large handful of baby spinach leaves
2 teaspoons chaat masala (see page 52)
Bengali tomato chutney (see page 162)

TIP
If making a big batch of pakoras, half cook them ahead of time in oil heated to 140°C. When you're ready to serve, finish off the pakoras in oil heated to 180°C.

TOMATO RASAM
WITH COCONUT AND PEA PANCAKES

A *rasam*, roughly translated as 'pepper water', is a southern Indian broth, reputed to blow away colds and encourage appetites. This recipe uses *masoor dal*, a quick-cooking lentil, but you could use skinned moong lentils, if you prefer. Fresh curry leaves are key to a *rasam's* distinctive citrussy flavour, although if you have to use dried leaves, don't fry them first – just add the dried leaves to the soup after it has been blended. I've used canned tomatoes for this recipe to ensure flavour, but do use fresh when they're in season.

In India, *rasam* is usually served on its own or with steamed rice cakes (*idlis*), but I've made pancakes, because they're quick and don't need special steaming moulds.

**MAKES 22 PANCAKES,
SERVES 4–6**

FOR THE RASAM
2 tablespoons sunflower oil
1 red onion, sliced
1 x 400g can of chopped
    tomatoes
¼ teaspoon ground turmeric
2 teaspoons caster sugar
½ teaspoon Kashmiri
    chilli powder
½ teaspoon coarsely ground
    black peppercorns
30g red lentils (*masoor
    dal*), rinsed
3 tablespoons chopped
    coriander

FOR THE TEMPERING
2 tablespoons sunflower oil
½ teaspoon black mustard seeds
about 15 fresh curry leaves
½ teaspoon chilli flakes
½ teaspoon cumin seeds
3 garlic cloves, finely chopped

FOR THE PANCAKES
1 x 400ml can of full-fat
    coconut milk
25g root ginger, peeled
    and roughly chopped
3 large garlic cloves, chopped

For the *rasam*, heat the oil in a medium pan over a medium-low heat. Add the onion and fry for about 8–10 minutes, until golden. Add the chopped tomatoes, turmeric, sugar, chilli powder, black pepper and lentils. Cook for 2–3 minutes, then pour over 1 litre of water, half cover the pan and continue cooking for 25 minutes, or until the lentils are soft. Leave to cool slightly, then blend the broth with a stick blender or in a liquidiser. Strain it into a clean pan, place over a low heat and bring back to a simmer.

Meanwhile, for the tempering, heat the oil in a small frying pan over a medium heat. Add the mustard seeds, then, after a few seconds, the curry leaves, chilli flakes, cumin seeds and chopped garlic. Fry the spices, stirring, for 1 minute, until the curry leaves darken and the spices release a warm, nutty aroma.

Add the fried spice mixture to the hot broth and simmer for a further 5 minutes to allow the flavours to mingle. Remove from the heat, cover and leave the flavours to steep while you make the pancakes.

Mix the coconut milk, ginger, garlic, peas, green chilli and coriander. Using a stick blender or liquidiser, blend everything until smooth.

Sift the rice flour, gram flour, salt and turmeric into a bowl and make a well in the centre. Pour in the spiced coconut milk and enough cold water (about 200ml) to make a slack batter – aim for the consistency of single cream. Set aside for about 20 minutes, then whisk in the bicarbonate of soda and add the onion. Add more water if the batter is too thick (you're still aiming for the consistency of single cream).

Heat a heavy griddle pan over a medium heat with 1 tablespoon of oil. Spoon small ladlefuls of batter onto the griddle, leaving space for them to spread as they cook. Using the base of the ladle, gently spread each one into a circle, about 6cm in diameter and 2.5mm thick. Spoon a little extra oil around the pancakes, cook them for 2–3 minutes on one side, then flip them over and cook for a further 2 minutes, until coloured on both sides. Transfer the cooked pancakes to a clean tea towel and fold it over to keep them warm.

Gently reheat the *rasam*, stir in the chopped coriander and serve straightaway with plain or buttered pancakes on the side.

50g fresh or frozen
   peas, blanched
1–2 green chillies,
   roughly chopped
3 tablespoons roughly
   chopped coriander
100g rice flour
100g gram flour
1 teaspoon fine sea salt
1 teaspoon ground turmeric
½ teaspoon bicarbonate of soda
1 red onion, finely diced
sunflower oil, for frying

ROASTED VERMICELLI
WITH GUNPOWDER SPICE MIX

What's not to love about a warming bowl of vermicelli, flecked with onions, potatoes, peanuts, peas and popped mustard seeds? I picked up this recipe over 30 years ago from my children's paediatrician in Delhi. Her cook had obviously had a good day, and while we were waiting to see the doctor, he came into the waiting room and handed out bowls of savoury vermicelli as if we were guests at a dinner party.

I've kept things simple with my choice of vegetables and chosen to let the crackling curry leaves, astringent spices and sweet coconut provide the character. The southern Indian gunpowder mix that finishes the dish is not quite as fiery as the name implies, but it does provide a texture contrast and works especially well with the sharpness of lime juice.

SERVES 4

Heat a karahi or wok over a medium heat. Add the vermicelli and dry-roast, stirring all the time, for 3–4 minutes, until it colours. Tip the vermicelli into a bowl and set aside.

Return the pan to the heat and add the oil. Add the peanuts and fry for 3–4 minutes, until they darken, then scoop them out and set aside.

Add the mustard seeds, cumin seeds and split Bengal gram to the hot oil left in the pan and cook for about 30 seconds, until the lentils colour and the cumin releases its nutty aroma. Stir in the curry leaves (they will probably splutter and crackle) and, after about 20 seconds, add the onions, ginger and green chillies. Cook over a low heat for 10 minutes, until the onions have softened.

Add the diced potato and turmeric, stir well, cover with a lid and continue cooking until the potatoes are just tender (about 7 minutes). Remove the lid, turn up the heat and fry the onions until golden.

Return the vermicelli to the pan, stir well and add enough cold water to barely cover the contents. Cover and simmer, without stirring, until the vermicelli has absorbed the liquid and is tender without being overcooked (about 5 minutes).

Stir in the peanuts, peas, coconut and coriander and add the lime juice. Sprinkle with gunpowder spice to taste before serving.

175g fine vermicelli (*seviyan*)
4–6 tablespoons sunflower oil
75g unsalted redskin peanuts
1½ teaspoons black
    mustard seeds
½ teaspoon cumin seeds
2 teaspoons split Bengal gram
    (*chana dal*)
about 30 fresh curry leaves
2 onions, finely sliced
50g root ginger, peeled
    and coarsely grated
2 green chillies, deseeded
    and finely chopped
300g floury potatoes, such as
    Maris Piper or King Edward,
    cut into 1cm cubes
½ teaspoon ground turmeric
50g fresh or frozen
    peas, blanched
50g frozen grated coconut,
    defrosted
2 tablespoons chopped
    coriander
juice of 2 limes
1–2 tablespoons gunpowder
    spice (see page 53)

BULGUR WHEAT AND CARDAMOM TIKKIS
WITH ORANGE-CARAMEL SAUCE

The creamy saffron filling in these Persian-inspired patties marks them as a speciality from Mughal palace kitchens. This recipe plays on the sweetness of warming spices, such as green cardamom in the tikki, saffron in the yoghurt and fennel seeds in the sauce. I've used strained Greek yoghurt here, which is easily available at supermarkets, but it's not difficult to make your own. Hang full-fat yoghurt in muslin so that the whey drips away and leaves behind a fresh curd cheese. The orange sauce is a modern departure from classic chutneys, but it does reflect the Mughals' penchant for using fruit in savoury dishes.

MAKES 20, SERVES 4–6

FOR THE SAFFRON YOGHURT
¼ teaspoon saffron strands
125g strained full-fat
   Greek yoghurt
pinch of caster sugar
salt and freshly ground
   black pepper

FOR THE TIKKIS
100g medium bulgur wheat
½ teaspoon black peppercorns
seeds from 8 green
   cardamom pods
1 blade of mace
pinch of caster sugar
100g red lentils (*masoor dal*)
25g root ginger, peeled
   and finely grated
25g ghee (see page 26)
   or unsalted butter
3 teaspoons fine semolina
1 red onion, finely diced
3 tablespoons chopped
   coriander
juice of 1 lime
about 500ml sunflower oil,
   for deep-frying

Make the yoghurt. Using a mortar and pestle, pound the saffron strands to a powder, then mix with 1 tablespoon of warm water. Leave the saffron to infuse for 1 hour or so, then add the mixture to the strained yoghurt with the sugar and season to taste. Set aside in the fridge.

To make the tikkis, put the bulgur wheat in a bowl and cover with boiling water. Seal the bowl with a lid and set the grains aside for 30 minutes to soak. Using a mortar and pestle, grind the peppercorns with the cardamom seeds, mace and sugar and set aside.

Meanwhile, put the red lentils and ginger in a pan and pour over enough water to cover. Place over a medium heat and bring to the boil, then reduce the heat and simmer for about 15–20 minutes, until the lentils are soft, dry and have absorbed all the cooking water. Add a splash more water to the pan if the lentils start to stick on the bottom. Stir in the ghee or butter and 1½ teaspoons of the peppercorn-cardamom-mace spice mixture, and leave to cool.

Spoon the bulgur wheat and cooled lentils into a food processor and blend until the mixture resembles a coarse paste. Transfer the mixture to a bowl and add the semolina, onion, coriander and enough lime juice to sharpen. Using wet hands, shape the mixture into 20 tikkis (patties), about 4cm in diameter, and flatten each in the palm of your hand to about 1cm thickness.

Put 1 teaspoon of the saffron yoghurt in the centre of each tikki, and using your fingers, gently pull the mixture around it to seal in the filling. Chill the tikkis for at least 30 minutes, to firm up.

Meanwhile, make the sauce. Put the sugar and glucose syrup in a small, heavy-bottomed pan with 125ml of water. Place over a low heat to dissolve the sugar, then increase the heat to medium-high and continue to cook until the mixture turns a deep caramel (about 4–5 minutes –

don't leave the pan unattended). Take the pan off the heat and add the orange juice and vinegar – take care as it will spit.

Return the pan to the heat to dissolve the caramel (about 1–2 minutes), then add the fennel seeds, chilli and a strip of pared orange rind. Cover and leave to one side to infuse for 15 minutes. Discard the orange rind and keep the sauce warm while you cook the tikkis.

Fill a large, wide, sturdy pan no more than two-thirds full with oil. The oil is ready for frying when it reaches 180°C on a food thermometer, or when a cube of bread dropped into the oil browns in 30 seconds. Then, add the tikkis, a few at a time, and deep-fry until golden all over (about 3 minutes). Serve with the warm orange sauce.

**FOR THE ORANGE-
CARAMEL SAUCE**

125g caster sugar

2 teaspoons glucose syrup

1 orange, pared rind of ½ and
  juice of whole

2 tablespoons white wine vinegar

1 teaspoon fennel seeds

1 red chilli, deseeded and
  finely chopped

CRISP-FRIED OKRA
WITH MANGO RELISH

Okra slivers dusted with spiced gram flour and fried until crisp take bar snacks to a whole new level. For the best results, choose firm, dry and young okra pods, topped and tailed. Wipe them clean with kitchen paper rather than running them under water, which makes them lose texture. In this recipe, it is the innocuous-looking carom seeds (known as *ajwain*) that punch far above their weight. A little goes a seriously long way, so don't be tempted to throw a few extra seeds into the mixture as it could easily turn bitter.

Choose unripe mangoes for the mango relish – those at Indian grocery stores are best, but you could use unripe supermarket varieties too.

SERVES 4–6

First, make the relish. Add the mango flesh to a small pan with just enough water to cover. Place over a low heat and simmer until most of the liquid has evaporated and the fruit has completely softened. Stir in enough sugar to sweeten – you might not need it all.

Sieve the mango pulp and then season little by little with the mint, cumin, black salt and chilli. Taste as you go – aim for a sweet-sour flavour. Store the relish in the fridge until needed – it will keep for 2–3 days.

Slice the okra into thin slivers on the diagonal. Sift the gram flour into a bowl with the turmeric, chilli powder and chaat masala or mango powder. Stir in the carom seeds or ground cumin and season generously with fine salt.

Just before you're ready to fry, coat the okra in the spiced gram flour (any sooner and the salt will make the okra soggy). Place the coated okra in a sieve and shake to disperse any excess flour.

To deep-fry, fill a large, wide, sturdy pan no more than two-thirds full with oil. The oil is ready for frying when it reaches 180°C on a food thermometer, or when a cube of bread dropped into the oil browns in 30 seconds.

Add the slivers of okra in batches, a few at a time, and deep-fry for about 3–4 minutes, until crisp. Remove each batch with a slotted spoon and set aside to drain on kitchen paper. Sprinkle with salt and serve straightaway with the mango relish.

300g okra, topped and tailed
100g gram flour
¾ teaspoon ground turmeric
1 teaspoon Kashmiri
    chilli powder
2 tablespoons chaat masala
    (see page 52) or mango
    powder (*amchoor*)
1 teaspoon carom seeds (*ajwain*)
    or 1 teaspoon roasted and
    ground cumin seeds
sunflower oil, for deep-frying
fine salt

FOR THE MANGO RELISH
350g green mangoes, peeled,
    halved and stoned
50g caster sugar
1 teaspoon dried mint
¾ teaspoon ground roasted
    cumin seeds
¼ teaspoon black salt
1 red chilli, deseeded and
    finely chopped

VADAS
GINGER AND GREEN CHILLI DOUGHNUTS

Shaped like doughnuts but made with lentils and seasoned with plenty of spice, these southern Indian fried dumplings (known as *vadas*) are traditionally served for breakfast, but also make a great light meal, especially when dunked in tamarind and vegetable lentils (see page 81).

In northern states, *vadas* aren't as highly spiced as they are in the south and are often soaked in warm water to soften them, before being cloaked in yoghurt. This dish, known as *dhai bhalla*, is especially popular at festival time, when it's often given a makeover and turned into a treat with the addition of chopped potatoes, pomegranate seeds and chaat masala, and served with relishes such as fresh coriander chutney (see page 163) and date and tamarind sauce (see page 167). I've used skinned, white urad lentils for this recipe, but you could use yellow moong lentils instead, or even a mixture of both.

MAKES 20–24, SERVES 6

250g skinned, white urad lentils (*dhuli urad dal*), soaked overnight
1 teaspoon ground roasted cumin seeds
½ teaspoon coarsely ground black peppercorns
1 heaped tablespoon sesame seeds
75g root ginger, peeled and chopped
about 15 fresh curry leaves
3–4 green chillies, deseeded and finely chopped
1 large onion, finely diced
1 small bunch of coriander, chopped
75–100g rice flour
1 teaspoon bicarbonate of soda
500ml sunflower oil, for oiling and deep-frying
tamarind and vegetable lentils (see page 81) or fresh coriander chutney (see page 163), to serve

Drain the lentils and put them in a food processor with the cumin, black pepper, sesame seeds, ginger, curry leaves and green chillies. Process until the lentils have broken down to a soft paste. You may need to add a little water.

Spoon the paste into a bowl and add in the onion and coriander. Stir in enough rice flour, little by little (you may not need all the flour), to bind the paste. Aim for a soft texture that you can mould with wet hands, rather than a dough-like consistency. Add the bicarbonate of soda when you are ready to shape and cook the mixture.

Oil your hands, then shape 1 portion of the paste into a ball, about the size of a small tangerine. Flatten it slightly on your palm and make a small hole in the centre – just like you would for a ring doughnut. Repeat the process with the remaining paste – you should get around 20–24 *vadas* from the mixture.

To deep-fry, fill a large, wide, sturdy pan no more than two-thirds full with oil. The oil is ready for frying when it reaches 180°C on a food thermometer, or when a cube of bread dropped into the oil browns in 30 seconds. Carefully lower each *vada* into the oil and deep-fry until golden all over (about 3–4 minutes on each side). Fry the *vadas* in batches, taking care not to overcrowd the pan. Serve hot with tamarind and vegetable lentils or fresh coriander chutney.

GHEE
TECHNIQUE

Cooking with ghee is an indulgence – it lends richness, has a lovely, buttery flavour and, like clarified butter, will heat to a high temperature without burning.

Traditionally, Indians make ghee with cream skimmed from the top of boiled milk, which is then churned into butter and cooked over a gentle heat until golden. The butter becomes ghee after it's strained and any sediment is removed.

Because ghee has no moisture or milk solids, it will keep at room temperature for 2–3 months without spoiling, but it is also relatively expensive to make. As a result, many Indian home cooks prefer to use a neutral-flavoured oil, such as sunflower or vegetable oil, for everyday cooking.

If you do cook with ghee, it's worth making your own. It's simple to do and the flavour is far superior to most commercial varieties, which are often let down by a metallic aftertaste.

250g unsalted butter

Heat the butter in a small, sturdy pan and cook over a low heat, without stirring, for 15–20 minutes, until the milk solids have browned and the butter is golden. Turn off the heat and leave the pan undisturbed for a few minutes.

Line a metal sieve with muslin or strong kitchen paper and place it over a heatproof bowl. Pour over the melted butter, taking care to leave the browned milk solids in the pan. Leave the ghee for a few minutes to drip into the bowl, and then pour it into a sterilised jar and keep it at room temperature for 2–3 months.

FIVE GOOD THINGS ABOUT USING GHEE

- It has a long shelf life.

- It heats to a high temperature without burning.

- It imbues a rich, buttery flavour to dishes.

- It is a natural fat with no additives.

- It is easy to make and you don't need to keep it chilled.

JACKET POTATOES
WITH SMOKED BLACK CARDAMOM BUTTER

The buttery topping on these jacket potatoes is scented with musky black cardamom, sweetened with caramelised dates and sharpened with a spike of ginger (the topping also makes a good spread for hot naan). Black cardamom isn't as well known as green cardamom, but it is a key ingredient in garam masala spice blends (see page 51), stridently spiced curries and fragrant pulaos. It is smoked over a fire pit and has a pronounced earthy flavour (green cardamoms impart sweeter and citrussy notes).

SERVES 6

To make the smoked butter, using a mortar and pestle, pound the cardamom seeds with the sugar until finely ground. Put the spice into a small food processor and add the peanuts and ginger. Process until the nuts are finely chopped.

Melt the butter in a pan and fry the chopped, spiced peanuts until they pick up colour and the butter begins to brown.

Take the pan off the heat and stir in the jaggery or sugar, dates, salt flakes, pepper and chilli powder. Transfer the butter mixture to a clean food processor and blend until it is combined, but still has texture. Spoon it into a metallic bowl and set aside.

Heat the oven to 220°C/200°C fan/gas mark 7. Rub the potatoes with the oil and then coat them generously with the salt. Bake the potatoes for about 40 minutes, or until tender when pierced with a knife.

While the potatoes are cooking, smoke the butter. Heat the charcoal over a gas flame (or in a very hot oven) until it glows. Make a small cup-shape out of the foil square, press it into the surface of the butter mixture and then add the empty cardamom pods.

When the charcoal is hot, carefully transfer it to the foil using tongs. Heat the ghee or clarified butter in a small pan and as soon as it begins to smoke, quickly pour it over the hot charcoal. Tightly cover the bowl with more foil to seal in the smoky, spiced aromas and set it aside for 30 minutes. Then, discard the foil cup and its contents.

Heat the grill to high. Split the jacket potatoes in half along their length, then squeeze over the juice of 1 lime. Spread a dollop of the smoked butter over the cut side of each halved potato and cook under the hot grill for 1–2 minutes, until the tops have caramelised. Cut the remaining lime into wedges and serve alongside the potatoes.

FOR THE SMOKED BUTTER
2 black cardamom pods, seeds removed and empty pods reserved
pinch of caster sugar
50g unsalted peanuts
20g root ginger, peeled and finely grated
125g unsalted butter
1 teaspoon jaggery or light brown soft sugar
3 pitted medjool dates, roughly chopped
1 teaspoon sea salt flakes
½ teaspoon coarsely ground black peppercorns
½ teaspoon Kashmiri chilli powder
2 tablespoons ghee (see page 26) or clarified butter

You will also need: 1 piece of lumpwood charcoal, about the size of a small walnut; and 1 square of strong foil, about the size of a large handkerchief, plus extra to seal the pan.

FOR THE POTATOES
6 floury potatoes, such as Maris Piper or King Edward
3 tablespoons sunflower oil
1 tablespoon salt
2 limes

ANDE BHUJIA
PUNJABI-STYLE SCRAMBLED EGGS

Order *ande bhujia* at a roadside *dhaba* in Punjab and you'll be treated to a hearty breakfast staple of eggs flecked with fried onions, softened tomatoes, green chillies and citrussy coriander. It's often partnered with a multi-layered paratha (see page 149) and a dab of mango pickle on the side.

Punjabis are not the only group with their own signature style of cooking eggs. The Parsees, originally from Persia, have myriad egg dishes in their repertoire. Their version of *ande bhujia* is called *akoori*, and includes ground turmeric and crushed garlic. It's served on buttered toast and topped with a tangle of crisp-fried potato straws.

SERVES 4

4 tablespoons sunflower oil
4 onions, diced
2 green chillies, deseeded
  and finely chopped
4 tomatoes, diced
½ teaspoon coarsely ground
  black peppercorns
50g ghee (see page 26)
  or unsalted butter
8 eggs, lightly beaten
2 tablespoons chopped
  coriander
sea salt flakes

Heat the oil in a large frying pan or wok over a medium heat. Add the onions and cook, stirring occasionally, for 8–10 minutes, until golden. Stir in the chillies, tomatoes and black pepper and continue cooking for a further 3–4 minutes, until the tomatoes have softened.

Reduce the heat to low and add the ghee or butter, followed by the beaten eggs. Leave undisturbed for 1–2 minutes, until the eggs have begun to set.

Gently lift the eggs from the bottom of the pan and season with sea salt flakes. Continue cooking and gently stirring for a further 1 minute for soft eggs, or 3–4 minutes if you prefer the eggs well set.

Stir in the chopped coriander and serve straightaway with buttered toast or parathas (see page 149), and perhaps a pickle of choice, such as green chilli pickle (see page 160), on the side.

BHEL PURI
PUFFED RICE SALAD WITH DATE AND TAMARIND SAUCE

This Gujarati-inspired *bhel puri* is a crunchy mix of puffed rice, peanuts, fried gram flour strands, herbs, spices and vegetables. The whole ensemble is cloaked in tamarind sauce and eaten straightaway before the rice loses its crisp texture. Its popularity extends across the country, while local adaptations lend regional flair. In Calcutta, *bhel puri* morphs into *jhal muri*, and is often drizzled with mustard oil; while in southern India, coconut shavings add tropical flavour. The tamarind sauce in this recipe is simmered with dates and jaggery and is typical of Gujarat's love of sweet and tart flavours.

Puffed rice, for most people in the West, is best known as a breakfast cereal. Not so in India, where it's enjoyed in both savoury and sweet snacks. The traditional way of making puffed rice is to put the grains in hot ovens, which have been filled with sand.

The intense heat makes the rice puff up in a similar way to corn kernels when they become popcorn. Indian grocery stores sell bags of *murmura* (puffed white rice grains), which keep for months, and *sev*, which are wispy strands of fried gram-flour batter and come in salted and chilli varieties. I prefer salted for this dish, because it doesn't detract from the sweet, tart and spicy flavours of the other ingredients.

SERVES 4–6

Heat the oven to 170°C/150°C fan/gas mark 3. Place the puffed rice in a large baking dish and bake for 10 minutes, or until crisp, then leave to cool.

Combine all the remaining ingredients, except the date and tamarind sauce and fresh coriander chutney. Stir through the baked rice, then add enough date and tamarind sauce to lightly coat. Streak the coriander chutney through the mixture, spoon into small dishes and serve straightaway, before the rice loses its crisp texture.

100g puffed rice (*murmura*)
50g fried gram-flour strands (*sev*)
200g waxy potatoes, scrubbed, boiled and diced
1 small red onion, diced
2 tomatoes, deseeded and diced
100g redskin unsalted peanuts, fried in 2 tablespoons sunflower oil
3 tablespoons chopped coriander
date and tamarind sauce (see page 167)
fresh coriander chutney (see page 163)

CHILLI CHEESE TOAST

Cheese toast is one of Britain and India's great culinary collaborations. A clubhouse favourite, it continues to be served in old-fashioned coffee houses, bars and cafés today. There's no set recipe, so you can turn the dial up or down on chilli levels, but chopped green chillies are integral to its appeal. The tomato topping here is a modern touch – it contrasts the big, bold flavours of spiced, melted cheese with sweet and mustardy notes. I like to think of this cheese toast as a revved-up version of Welsh rarebit – serve it with a cumin-dusted poached egg, if you're feeling extra peckish.

SERVES 6–8

8 slices of white bread
50g unsalted butter
175g mature Cheddar
   cheese, grated
1 small red onion, diced
1–2 green chillies, deseeded
   and finely chopped
2 tablespoons chopped
   coriander
1 teaspoon ground roasted
   cumin seeds
½ teaspoon coarsely ground
   black pepper
¾ teaspoon Kashmiri
   chilli powder

FOR THE TOMATO TOPPING
2 tablespoons sunflower oil
½ teaspoon black mustard seeds
200g cherry tomatoes, halved
pinch of caster sugar
juice of ½ lime

Heat the grill to high. Put the bread slices on the grill pan and toast them on one side. Remove from the grill and butter the untoasted side of each slice. Mix the grated cheese with the onion, green chillies and chopped coriander. Season the cheese mixture with cumin, black pepper and chilli powder, and thickly spread the mixture over the buttered side of the bread. Cook the slices under a hot grill for about 2 minutes, until the cheese has melted and is golden and bubbling.

While the bread is under the grill prepare the tomato topping. Heat the oil in a small karahi, wok or frying pan over a medium heat. Add the mustard seeds and fry for about 30 seconds, or until they stop sizzling. Stir in the tomatoes and sugar and cook over a high heat for a further 30 seconds, then stir in the lime juice.

Spoon a few tomatoes and the mustard-seed-speckled oil over each cheese toast and serve straightaway.

GREEN PEA AND POTATO SAMOSAS

There's no better food to eat on the go than a hot samosa filled with crushed spiced potatoes, studded with garden peas. Simple ingredients make the best foundation for showcasing the versatility of spice. In this recipe, it's the fruitiness of mango powder, cumin's nutty flavour and the warming notes of garam masala that shine through.

Samosas in northern and central India have a shortcrust-like casing. However, in Muslim areas, such as in parts of Ahmedabad in Gujarat, the pastry is filo-like and the samosas are smaller. Indian shops in the West sell packets of frozen samosa pastry strips, known as pads, which I've used for this recipe – they're easy to use and already cut into sheets that are just the right size for making cocktail samosas. I like to double up the pastry strips so that the samosas stay crisp for longer after frying.

MAKES 24 SMALL SAMOSAS, SERVES 6

Heat the 2 tablespoons of oil in a large pan over a medium-low heat. Add the onion and ginger and fry for about 8–10 minutes, until softened. Stir in the potato and continue cooking, with the lid on, for about 10 minutes, until the potato is tender. Add the chillies, cumin, garam masala and mango powder and cook for a further 1 minute. Turn off the heat and stir in the blanched peas and then the chopped mint, and leave the mixture to cool.

Mix the flour with enough water to make a slack paste – you'll use this to seal the pastry-strip edges together.

Lay 3 samosa strips side by side on your work surface (if you're using filo pastry sheets, cut the sheets into strips measuring roughly 21cm x 7cm). Top each strip with another, to give you 3 casings of double thickness. Spoon a heaped teaspoonful of the pea mixture onto the top left corner of each of the casings. One by one, fold each casing over the filling so that you have 3 pocket-shaped triangles, folding back and forth to create 3 neat samosa packages. Seal any open edges with the flour-and-water paste, then repeat the process with the remaining pastry strips and filling.

To deep-fry, fill a large, wide, sturdy pan no more than two-thirds full with oil. The oil is ready for frying when it reaches 180°C on a food thermometer, or when a cube of bread dropped into the oil browns in 30 seconds. Deep-fry the samosas in batches until crisp and golden all over – about 7 minutes per batch. Remove the samosas from the oil using a slotted spoon and set aside to drain on kitchen paper. Serve straightaway with your chosen chutneys.

2 tablespoons sunflower oil, plus extra for deep-frying
1 red onion, finely chopped
25g root ginger, peeled and finely chopped
1 floury potato, such as Maris Piper or King Edward, cut into 5mm dice
2 green chillies, deseeded and finely chopped
1 teaspoon ground roasted cumin seeds
1 teaspoon garam masala (see page 51)
2 teaspoons mango powder (amchoor)
250g fresh or frozen green peas, blanched
2 tablespoons chopped mint leaves
2 tablespoons plain flour
40–44 samosa strips or a 270g packet of filo pastry sheets
chutney of your choice (see pages 161–167), to serve

CHAAT MASALA FRUIT SALAD

There's no single word in the English language that describes the spectrum of flavours delivered by *chaat*. However, in India, it's the emotive-sounding *chatpata* that evokes myriad explosive tastes and textures. If you feel like eating something *chatpata*, the assumption is that it's *chaat*, or at a least a spicy crunchy snack.

This *chaat* is a spicy fruit salad with crisp cucumber and tamarind-glazed butternut squash, cloaked in a lime-drenched dressing. (You could use sweet potatoes instead of the squash.) The best fruit *chaats* leave a lingering slow burn of chilli on the lips, but I've erred on the side of caution. If you want an extra hit of heat, leave the seeds in the chilli.

SERVES 6–8

200g fresh pineapple, cubed
1 mango, flesh cubed
1 pear, peeled and cubed
½ cucumber, peeled, deseeded
  and cubed
1 red chilli, deseeded and
  finely chopped
1 teaspoon ground roasted
  cumin seeds
2 teaspoons mango
  powder (*amchoor*)
½ teaspoon black salt
15g root ginger, peeled and
  finely grated
½ teaspoon coarsely ground
  black peppercorns
2 tablespoons chopped
  mint leaves
juice of 1 lime
1–2 teaspoons caster sugar,
  if needed

FOR THE BUTTERNUT SQUASH

2 tablespoons wet tamarind pulp,
  seedless (see page 158)
1 tablespoon jaggery or light
  brown soft sugar
½ teaspoon dried red chilli flakes
2 tablespoons sunflower oil
200g butternut squash,
  peeled, deseeded and cut
  into 2cm chunks

Start with the butternut squash. Heat the oven to 200°C/180°C fan/ gas mark 6.

Mix the tamarind pulp with the jaggery or sugar, chilli flakes and oil and stir in the cubed butternut squash.

Line a roasting tin with baking parchment, add the squash and roast it for about 15 minutes, until the glaze is sticky and the squash is tender. Remove from the oven and leave to cool.

While the squash is cooling, make the salad. Combine the pineapple, mango, pear, cucumber and red chilli in a serving bowl. Stir in the ground cumin, mango powder, black salt, ginger, pepper and mint and then sharpen with lime juice to taste. Leave the fruit to steep for 10 minutes, then stir in the cooled butternut squash. The *chaat* should be tart with a hint of sweetness – stir in a little caster sugar, if needed.

SPINACH AND FIG TIKKIS

These elegant patties, made with ground spinach mixed with chopped figs, are seasoned with sharp, green chilli, citrussy cardamom and astringent ginger, and originate from the Middle East. Karunesh Khanna, head chef at London's fine-dining Tamarind restaurant, introduced me to these more than a decade ago, and I've been making versions of them ever since. Sometimes I use chopped dried apricots instead of figs, or I coat the tikkis in white poppy seeds if I've run short on sesame seeds. I've used some artistic licence and included a crunchy, sesame-seed coating in these tikkis. The Kashmiri walnut yoghurt accompaniment has a surprise chilli kick.

MAKES 32, SERVES 8

First, make the walnut yoghurt. Put the walnuts in a food processor and process until finely chopped. Add the remaining ingredients and then blend until smooth. Set aside so that the flavours mellow while you make the tikkis.

Heat a dry, heavy pan or flameproof casserole over a high heat. Add the spinach and cook for 1 minute or so, until the spinach has wilted. Transfer the spinach to a plate and pat dry with kitchen paper. When the leaves are cool enough to handle, finely chop them and set aside.

Roast the gram flour in a separate, dry pan over a medium heat for 2–3 minutes, stirring all the time, until the flour darkens. Tip it onto a plate and leave to cool.

Heat the 4 tablespoons of oil in a small frying pan over a medium-low heat. Add the onion and cook for about 8–10 minutes, until it is soft, but not coloured. Add the garlic, garam masala, ground cumin, ground cardamom-sugar and green chillies, and continue cooking for a further 1 minute. Add the chopped spinach and cook over a high heat for a further 3–4 minutes, until all the moisture has evaporated and the spinach is quite dry. Stir in the chopped figs, mashed potato and roasted gram flour, then take the pan off the heat and leave the mixture to cool before chilling it for 20–30 minutes.

Using wet hands, shape the mixture into discs, about 4cm in diameter and 1cm thick – you should get 32 tikkis from the mixture. Coat each one on both sides with the sesame seeds.

Heat a 2cm depth of oil in a frying pan over a medium heat. In batches fry the tikkis for 2–3 minutes on each side, until the sesame has coloured. Drain each batch on kitchen paper while you cook the next. Once all the tikkis are cooked, serve them warm with the walnut yoghurt.

600g baby spinach leaves
2 tablespoons gram flour
4 tablespoons sunflower oil,
  plus extra for frying
1 onion, diced
4 garlic cloves, crushed
½ teaspoon garam masala
  (see page 51)
½ teaspoon ground roasted
  cumin seeds
seeds from 3 green cardamom
  pods, ground with a pinch
  of sugar
1–2 green chillies,
  finely chopped
150g soft dried figs, chopped
1 floury potato, such as Maris
  Piper or King Edward, peeled,
  boiled and mashed
4–6 tablespoons sesame seeds,
  for coating

FOR THE WALNUT YOGHURT
50g walnuts
1 banana shallot, chopped
2 green chillies, chopped
1 tablespoon dried mint leaves
¼ teaspoon Kashmiri
  chilli powder
1 tablespoon chopped coriander
125g full-fat Greek yoghurt

RAJASTHANI SLOW-COOKED POTATOES

Green chillies and leafy coriander have starring roles in this Rajasthani dish. The long, slow cooking softens the chillies and melds them into the tangy yoghurt masala. I've used Charlotte potatoes here, because they hold their shape well, but you could opt for floury varieties, such as Maris Piper or King Edward, which are excellent for soaking up spiced masala. Much of Rajasthan is challenged with arid landscapes and, traditionally, vegetables were cooked in yoghurt to conserve scarce water supplies.

A couple of points on ingredients: pale green, Turkish chillies give a mild flavour that is especially suitable for this dish. Avoid skinny bird's eye chillies, which are too fiery. Buy big bunches of citrussy coriander from Asian grocery stores, if you can, as the leaves will have a fuller flavour than supermarket offerings. And use full-fat yoghurt, which is more stable than reduced fat when heated.

Serve this rich potato dish with a simple tarka dal (see page 85), flatbreads and chilled cucumber wedges sharpened with a squeeze of lime and then dusted with a little ground cumin and salt.

SERVES 4

30g coriander, roughly chopped
350g full-fat Greek yoghurt
1 tablespoon gram flour
¾ teaspoon ground roasted
   cumin seeds
50g ghee (see page 26) or
   3–4 tablespoons sunflower oil
1 onion, thinly sliced
20g root ginger, peeled and cut
   into thin matchsticks
3 garlic cloves, thinly sliced
50g mild green chillies,
   deseeded and thickly sliced
600g Charlotte potatoes,
   scrubbed and halved

Heat the oven to 170°C/150°C fan/gas mark 3.

Put the coriander, yoghurt, gram flour and cumin in a food processor and blend until smooth.

Heat the ghee or oil in a sturdy medium flameproof casserole over a medium-low heat. Add the onion, ginger, garlic and green chillies and cook for 8–10 minutes, until the onion has softened.

Add the coriander and yoghurt mixture and 200ml of hot water to the pan and bring to a simmer, stirring all the time. Stir in the halved potatoes, then cover the casserole with foil and a tight-fitting lid and cook in the oven for 1½ hours, until the potatoes are tender and the masala has thickened.

PORIYAL
BEETROOT WITH CURRY LEAVES AND COCONUT

This is a southern Indian *poriyal*, which is similar to stir-fry and made with grated or chopped vegetables. *Poriyals* are quick to cook and give fridge-foraged vegetables a refreshing, makeover. I've used beetroot here because its sweetness works well with the pungency of popped mustard seeds, crackling curry leaves and dried red chillies. Other options could include shredded cabbage, sliced green beans, diced carrots or broad beans. Crunchy fried lentils are an essential feature of this dish and, although the recipe calls for only a teaspoonful, their crisp texture and nutty flavour make their presence felt.

Fresh coconut is an everyday ingredient in Keralan dishes, and in this recipe the coconut is grated and stirred into the *poriyal* at the end of cooking. Serve this dish with tamarind and vegetable lentils (see page 81) and rice (see page 136) for a delicious, light and nourishing meal.

SERVES 4

Put the beetroot in a medium pan, cover with cold water and simmer over a low heat for about 40 minutes, until tender. Drain and leave the beetroot to cool. Once the beetroot are cool enough to handle, peel and cut them into 2cm cubes and set aside. (Wear gloves as you handle them to prevent staining your fingers pink.)

Heat the oil in a karahi or wok over a medium heat. Add the mustard seeds and fry for about 30 seconds, until they stop spluttering. Add the white lentils, cumin seeds, chilli flakes, curry leaves and ginger. Cook for a further 1 minute, until the lentils have browned, then add the onion and green chilli. Reduce the heat to low and cook for about 8–10 minutes, until the onions are soft but not coloured.

Stir in the beetroot, then add a generous splash of water and cook for about 5 minutes, until the liquid evaporates. Stir in most of the coconut, reserving 1 tablespoon to sprinkle over the beetroot before serving.

400g even-sized small beetroot, leaves removed
3 tablespoons coconut or sunflower oil
1½ teaspoons black mustard seeds
1 teaspoon skinned, white urad lentils (*dhuli urad dal*)
½ teaspoon cumin seeds
½ teaspoon dried red chilli flakes
about 30 fresh curry leaves
20g root ginger, peeled and finely grated
1 red onion, finely diced
1 green chilli, slit (stem intact)
50g frozen grated coconut, defrosted

FENNEL-SPICED BABY TURNIPS

Turnips are at their best during the winter months across northern India, and most Punjabis are familiar with them in salads or as pickles. I picked up this recipe from Gulshan, a talented home cook, who works on the checkout at my local supermarket in London. We often share recipes – it's her way of staying in touch with her homeland while she's thousands of kilometres away. She'll chat to me in Punjabi: 'English turnips are too strong,' she sniffs, 'so choose only the smallest ones, and remember to salt them, which will draw out bitter juices.'

She's absolutely right about the salting process. This small act transforms this humble root into a homely, comforting and utterly delicious vegetable, which, when cooked with masala, tastes as good with chapatis (see page 148) as it does with a slice of buttered white bread. The tartness of ground mango and the sweet warmth of fennel seeds are truly outstanding seasonings for this simply prepared vegetable. If ever a dish can recreate a taste of 'back home', this is it.

SERVES 3–4

500g baby turnips, peeled
    and cut into 2.5cm dice
30g ghee (see page 26)
    or unsalted butter
1 onion, diced
20g root ginger, peeled and
    finely chopped
4 garlic cloves, finely chopped
1 teaspoon ground roasted
    coriander seeds
¼ teaspoon ground turmeric
½ teaspoon Kashmiri
    chilli powder
½ teaspoon ground roasted
    fennel seeds
1 green chilli, deseeded and
    finely chopped
1 teaspoon mango
    powder (amchoor)
1 tablespoon chopped coriander

Generously salt the diced turnips and set aside for 1 hour to draw out any bitter juices. Rinse off the salt and pat them dry with kitchen paper.

Heat the ghee or butter in a karahi or wok over a medium-low heat. Add the onion and fry for about 8–10 minutes, until golden. Stir in the ginger and garlic and, after 1 minute, add the turnips, ground coriander, turmeric, chilli powder, ground fennel and green chilli. Cover the pan and cook over a gentle heat for 15 minutes, stirring occasionally, until the turnips start to become tender.

Add the mango powder and continue cooking, with the lid on, for a further 15–20 minutes, until the turnips are soft and start to break down. (Add a splash of water to prevent sticking, if needed.) Crush some of the pieces against the side of the pan with the back of a wooden spoon, then stir in the chopped coriander.

KASHMIRI CHILLI AND CARDAMOM POTATOES

This variation on a classic dish from Rajasthan is made with relatively few ingredients by Indian standards. Pounded chillies are blended with yoghurt and cooked with caramelised onions and shedloads of garlic in ghee. Whole black cardamom is the lead spice here and its naturally smoky flavour is a good match for the robustly flavoured masala and softened potatoes.

This is not a dish for the faint-hearted. I've opted for Kashmiri chillies (milder than the traditional *mathania* used in abundance throughout Rajasthan), which also bring a lovely reddish hue to the finished dish. Don't be too finicky about removing every seed – a couple of stray ones are good for emboldening the masala. Serve these potatoes with a crisp salad, such as mixed salad (see page 156), cooling yoghurt and chapatis (see page 148).

SERVES 4–6

Using scissors, snip the tops off the dried chillies and shake to remove the seeds. Put the chillies in a heatproof bowl and cover with boiling water. Leave to soak for 30 minutes, drain, then blend the rehydrated chillies in a food processor with the yoghurt, turmeric and coriander. (Alternatively, finely chop the drained chillies and mix them with the other ingredients.)

Heat the ghee or butter in a sturdy medium flameproof casserole over a medium heat. Add the onions and cardamom pods and fry for 8–10 minutes, until the onions are golden. Stir in the bay leaves or cinnamon and garlic and cook for a further 5 minutes, until the garlic is softened. Heat the oven to 160°C/140°C fan/gas mark 2–3.

Add the potatoes and yoghurt-and-chilli masala and cook over a medium heat for 3–5 minutes, until almost all the yoghurt has evaporated. Add a splash of water if the mixture looks like catching on the bottom of the pan.

Pour over enough hot water to barely cover the bottom of the casserole, then cover with foil and a tight-fitting lid. Transfer the casserole to the oven for 45 minutes, or until the potatoes are tender and the masala has thickened.

8 dried Kashmiri chillies
200g full-fat Greek yoghurt
¾ teaspoon ground turmeric
2 teaspoons ground roasted
  coriander seeds
100g ghee (see page 26)
  or unsalted butter
3 onions, thinly sliced
3 black cardamom pods, pierced
  with the point of a knife
4 Indian bay leaves (*tej patta*) or
  4cm cinnamon stick
1 large garlic bulb, cloves
  separated, peeled and
  shredded
750g floury potatoes, such as
  Maris Piper or King Edward,
  peeled and cut into 2cm chunks

SPICES

TEN TIPS FOR GRINDING AND FRYING SPICES AND MASALAS

- For best results use a mortar and pestle for grinding spices. The pestle bruises the spices, which draws out their volatile oils. An electric grinder splices them with its sharp blade, which doesn't give such an aromatic result. However, it is a much quicker process.

- It's easier to grind small quantities of spice with a porcelain or stone mortar and pestle than in an electric grinder.

- Coffee grinders are great for taking the hard work out of pulverising spices. However, it does mean that your machine won't be any good for coffee beans afterwards.

- It's a good idea to break up larger sticks, such as cinnamon, before grinding in an electric grinder, as they may get jammed in the blades.

- Grinding cardamom seeds in a mortal and pestle is much easier if you add a pinch of sugar to the mortar – the sugar acts as an abrasive.

- Lightly roasting spices makes it easier to break them down when grinding.

- Cumin seeds are dry-roasted in a small, heavy pan, preheated over a medium heat. Stir the seeds as they roast, to prevent scorching. They'll start to release a nutty aroma after about 30 seconds, but don't take them off the heat now, continue cooking them for a further 30 seconds, until they darken and the first wisps of smoke start wafting up from the pan. If you remove the cumin too early, it won't have developed its full flavour. Tip the seeds out of the hot pan and onto a plate to cool before grinding.

- When frying spices, it's important to get the temperature of the oil just right. Heat the oil over a medium heat for best results. If it gets too hot, the spices will scorch and become bitter. If the oil is too cool, they will not release their aroma and flavour. Ideally, spices should sizzle as soon as they are added to the oil.

- It's a good idea to fry spices for tarkas (the finishing ingredients for dal) in a small frying pan, karahi or wok, rather than in a large frying pan. The smaller bases of these pans make it easier to control the heat of the oil and prevent spices from burning.

- Many Indian recipes call for pounded pastes made from onion, ginger and garlic. It's a good idea to do this in a food processor or with a stick blender, adding a little hot water, so that the ingredients are blended to a purée.

GARAM MASALA

Garam masala is an aromatic spice blend that has many interpretations and remains an essential seasoning across southern Asia. This version is from northern India. It includes *shahi jeera*, also known as 'royal cumin', which has a characteristic smoky and astringent flavour, which makes it quite distinct from regular cumin.

MAKES 100G

Tip all the spices into an electric grinder and process until finely ground. (You can use a mortar and pestle for this if you don't have a grinder.)

Sift the ground spices and store in a tightly lidded jam jar – the blend will keep for about 2 months. If you're not likely to use it all up in that time, freeze the garam masala in an airtight plastic box – it will keep frozen for at least 6 months.

seeds from about 50g black cardamom pods (enough to provide 25g seeds)
25g cinnamon sticks, broken into pieces
25g whole black peppercorns
10g *shahi jeera* or 15g regular cumin seeds
2 large blades of mace
7g cloves (about 1 teaspoon)
¼ whole nutmeg

FIVE WAYS WITH GARAM MASALA

- For southern Indian garam masala, roast the spices above (use regular cumin rather than *shahi jeera*) in a small, dry pan with 2 star anise, about 30 fresh curry leaves and 2 teaspoons of black mustard seeds.

- Stir garam masala into soups for an aromatic flavour. Half a teaspoon, added to vegetables, as they soften, will lend a subtle fragrance to 500ml of soup.

- Fold 1 tablespoon of melted butter and 1 teaspoon of garam masala into piping-hot, boiled rice for 4–6 people.

- Season fried nuts while they are still hot with garam masala, salt and chilli powder.

- For a perfumed Mughal-style spice blend, replace the black cardamom with green cardamom seeds and add 2 tablespoons of dried rose petals before grinding.

CHAAT MASALA

This cornucopia of spices is crammed with big flavours. Here, the sulphurous aromas of quarried black salt and asafoetida contrast the sour fruitiness of mango powder and the lingering warmth of black pepper, chillies and cumin. Carom seeds bring pungency and boast a flavour that straddles lovage and thyme.

MAKES 75G

1 tablespoon cumin seeds
1 tablespoon black peppercorns
½ teaspoon carom seeds (*ajwain*)
1½ tablespoons dried mint leaves
small pinch of ground
   asafoetida (*heeng*)
¾ tablespoon ground black salt
1 teaspoon fine sea salt
3 tablespoons mango
   powder (*amchoor*)
1 teaspoon ground ginger
½ teaspoon grated nutmeg
½ teaspoon Kashmiri chilli powder

Roast the cumin, peppercorns and carom seeds in a dry pan over a medium heat for 1 minute, until the spices are fragrant. Take the pan off the heat and stir in the dried mint and asafoetida. Use a mortar and pestle or an electric grinder to pound everything to a powder, then add both salts, along with the mango powder, ground ginger, grated nutmeg and chilli powder. Store in an airtight jar. It'll keep at room temperature for 2–3 months, or for 6 months in the freezer.

FIVE WAYS WITH CHAAT MASALA

- Sprinkle generously over roast potatoes 5 minutes before they are ready and finish with a squeeze of lime.

- Season honey-roasted root vegetables, such as parsnip and carrots, with chaat masala before serving.

- Sprinkle chaat masala, chopped mint and a squeeze of lime or lemon over assorted chopped fruit to give it a refreshing lift.

- Dust French fries with salt, vinegar and tart-tasting chaat masala.

- Enliven a bowl of plain yoghurt with chaat masala and chopped herbs.

GUNPOWDER SPICE MIX

Known as *podi*, gunpowder enlivens a plain meal with nutty, warming and fiery flavours. Its coarse texture draws on a blend of roasted lentils, coconut, peanuts, pounded spice and plenty of dried red chilli.

MAKES 100G

Heat a small, sturdy frying pan over a low heat. Add both types of lentil, along with the sesame seeds, asafoetida (if using) and desiccated coconut. Roast everything together, stirring all the time, for just over 1 minute, until the lentils and coconut pick up colour. Remove from the heat and turn everything out onto a plate and leave to cool.

Wipe the pan clean with kitchen paper and add the oil. Place over a medium heat and add the dried red chillies. Fry for a few seconds, then add the peanuts and fry, stirring all the time, until they have browned. Transfer the chillies and peanuts to the spice mix, leaving any oil in the pan.

Add the salt and jaggery or sugar to the chilli, peanut and spice mixture, then leave to cool. Transfer the mixture to an electric grinder or mortar and pestle and grind to a coarse powder. Spoon the gunpowder spice into a dry, clean jar. Store at room temperature away from sunlight. It will keep for 2–3 months.

1 tablespoon skinned, white urad lentils *(dhuli urad dal)*
1 tablespoon split Bengal gram *(chana dal)*
1 tablespoon sesame seeds
small pinch of ground asafoetida *(heeng)*, optional
2 tablespoons desiccated coconut
1 tablespoon sunflower oil
5 dried Kashmiri chillies
1 tablespoon unsalted peanuts, skinned
1 teaspoon fine sea salt
1 teaspoon jaggery or light brown soft sugar

FIVE WAYS WITH GUNPOWDER SPICE MIX

- Use it as a shortcut for imbuing flavour into a masala when you are short of time.

- It's a great seasoning for dal and also gives everyday soups a southern Indian twist.

- Mix it into softened butter and use as a filling for jacket potatoes.

- Add it to grated cheese for puff-pastry cheese straws.

- Mix it with fresh breadcrumbs and scatter over macaroni or cauliflower cheese before baking or grilling until crisp. It's also good for chilli-stuffed mushrooms (see page 141).

PANCH PHORAN

This whole spice mix is a Bengali and Bangladeshi speciality. Fry a small quantity in oil at the start or end of cooking to release the aromatics (as little as 1 teaspoon in a vegetable dish to serve four people is all you'll need). The heat releases sweet, astringent and pungent flavours and provides distinctive seasoning for chutneys, dals and a range of masalas.

MAKES 2 TABLESPOONS

2 teaspoons cumin seeds
2 teaspoons black mustard seeds
2 teaspoons fennel seeds
1 teaspoon nigella seeds
1 teaspoon fenugreek seeds

Combine the raw spices in a small bowl, then transfer to a lidded jar to store at room temperature for 6–8 months.

FIVE WAYS WITH PANCH PHORON

- Use it to flavour roasted butternut squash. Drop 1 teaspoon into hot olive oil and sizzle for about 30 seconds before mixing it with the squash for roasting.

- Add it to tomato-based sauces, ketchups, chutneys and soups, frying the spices in oil before you begin.

- Fry 1 teaspoon in hot olive oil for 30 seconds, then add wilted greens, such as spinach, cabbage or chard. Stir-fry the leaves over a high heat for 1 minute, then serve straightaway.

- When making a tarka for dal, fry 1 teaspoon in the oil before adding the rest of the ingredients.

- Add a new dimension to salad dressings – sizzle the spices in olive oil, then add to the dressing and leave it to mellow for 1 hour before using.

SAMBAR POWDER

All Indian grocery stores sell *sambar* powder. Although it's convenient to use shop-bought varieties, there's something deeply satisfying about roasting and grinding your own spice blend at home. A mortar and pestle provides best results, but an electric grinder does the job too, and is an invaluable time-saver.

MAKES 4–6 TABLESPOONS

Heat a sturdy frying pan over a low heat. Add both types of lentil and red chillies and dry-roast, stirring all the time, for about 2 minutes, until they darken. Add all the remaining ingredients apart from the turmeric, and continue cooking for about 1 minute, or until the spices are fragrant. Take the pan off the heat and stir in the turmeric.

Grind the spices to a powder using a mortar and pestle or electric grinder and store in an airtight jar. This spice blend will keep for 1 month at room temperature or for 6 months in the freezer.

1 teaspoon skinned, white urad
    lentils (*dhuli urad dal*)
2 teaspoons split Bengal gram
    (*chana dal*)
4 dried red Kashmiri chillies
½ teaspoon fenugreek seeds
1 teaspoon black peppercorns
1 teaspoon coriander seeds
1 teaspoon black mustard seeds
2 teaspoons cumin seeds
pinch of ground
    asafoetida (*heeng*)
about 30 fresh curry leaves
1 teaspoon ground turmeric

FIVE WAYS WITH SAMBAR POWDER

- Add to stir-fries for a richly aromatic southern Indian flavour.

- Stir it into fruit-based dishes, such as ginger-spiced pineapple and tomato curry (see page 101) or add it to southern-style mango curry (see page 98), for extra chilli heat.

- Stir a little into the dressing or mayonnaise of a potato salad.

- Sprinkle over hard-boiled eggs as a punchy seasoning, or use it in the potatoes for spiced potato Scotch eggs (see page 132).

- Use it to season batters – 1 tablespoon added to 150g plain flour or gram flour will provide a lively kick.

RED PEPPERS
IN TOMATO AND CUMIN MASALA

This simple recipe has much in common with Mediterranean stews and features a homely mixture of softened onions, peppers, garlic and tomatoes. The addition of chilli powder, garam masala and Indian bay leaves (*tej patta*) marks it as Indian, but it's a dish that would work well with pasta as well as rice. I sometimes add cubed paneer to it just before serving – if you are using the shop-bought variety, soak it in hot water first. Red peppers have a natural sweetness, but you could use sharper-tasting green peppers, if you prefer.

Although Indian bay leaves look similar to European ones, they are not interchangeable. *Tej patta* have a pronounced clove-cinnamon flavour, so if you can't get hold of them, substitute with a cinnamon or cassia stick instead.

SERVES 4

50g ghee (see page 26)
   or unsalted butter
2 onions, thickly sliced
3 garlic cloves, shredded
2 large red peppers, deseeded
   and thickly sliced
4 Indian bay leaves (*tej patta*)
   or a 2cm cinnamon stick
4 large tomatoes,
   roughly chopped
1 teaspoon Kashmiri
   chilli powder
½ teaspoon garam masala
   (see page 51)
1 teaspoon ground roasted
   cumin seeds
1 teaspoon caster sugar

Heat the ghee or butter in a medium pan over a medium-low heat. Add the onions and cook for 10 minutes, until soft but not coloured. Add the garlic, cook for a further 5 minutes, until softened, then stir in the peppers and bay leaves or cinnamon. Cook for a further 10 minutes, until the peppers soften.

Stir in the tomatoes, chilli powder, garam masala, cumin and sugar. Cover the pan and simmer for 15 minutes, or until the tomatoes have softened and thickened and the peppers are tender.

MALAI PYAZ
RAJASTHANI ONIONS IN CREAM

Onions don't often feature as a standalone ingredient – they're usually the foundation for curries and masalas, or the supporting act for other vegetables. Not so in Rajasthan, where onions simmered in spiced cream (*malai pyaz*) are a local speciality. There's no garlic or ginger in this recipe: instead tart mango powder, warming fennel seeds, pungent fenugreek leaves and sharp chillies all contrast the sweetness of creamy, slow-cooked onions.

Although dried fenugreek leaves (*kasuri methi*) aren't that well known outside of India, their intense and bitter flavour is a splendid foil for the sweetness of other spices. Resist the urge to use more than the recipe indicates – a little really does go a long way. Lightly roasting the leaves for a few seconds freshens the flavour and crisps the texture.

SERVES 4–6

Dry-roast the dried fenugreek leaves in a small frying pan over a medium heat, stirring all the time, until they release a toasted aroma – this only takes a few seconds. Transfer the leaves to a plate and crumble into a powder. Leave to one side.

Heat the ghee or oil in a karahi or wok over a medium heat. Add the cumin and fennel seeds and fry for about 1 minute, stirring all the time, until fragrant.

Stir in the onions and green chillies, cover the pan and cook over a low heat for about 20 minutes, until softened. Remove the lid, increase the heat and fry for about 3–4 minutes, until the onions are golden.

Stir in the turmeric, chilli powder, ground coriander, mango powder, sugar and crumbled fenugreek leaves. Continue cooking for a further 1–2 minutes, then pour in the cream, bring to a simmer and cook for a further 30 seconds. Add the chopped coriander and serve.

2 teaspoons dried fenugreek
   leaves (*kasuri methi*)
50g ghee (see page 26)
   or 3–4 tablespoons
   sunflower oil
1 teaspoon cumin seeds
1 teaspoon fennel seeds
750g onions, thickly sliced
2 green chillies, slit
   and deseeded
¼ teaspoon ground turmeric
½ teaspoon Kashmiri
   chilli powder
1 teaspoon roasted ground
   coriander seeds
1 teaspoon mango powder
   (*amchoor*)
½ teaspoon caster sugar
200ml single cream
2 tablespoons chopped
   coriander

BAINGAN BHARTA
SMOKY AUBERGINE MASH

Aubergines are indigenous to India and this rustic mash, known as *baingan bharta*, is a regular feature of Punjabi meals. Traditionally, aubergines are roasted over an open fire, then the pulp is fried in ghee to a deep, russet brown with onions, ginger, garlic, tomatoes and spices. Surprisingly, the ordinary gas hob does the job pretty well, too. Choose medium-sized, plump aubergines with smooth, purple skin. As the skin chars, the flesh collapses into a velvety mash. Sadly, you don't get the same degree of smokiness if you're using an electric stove, but you could rub the aubergine with oil and roast it in an oven on its hottest setting for about 40 minutes, until tender.

SERVES 6

2 large aubergines
50g ghee (see page 26)
   or unsalted butter
2 onions, diced
25g root ginger, peeled and
   finely grated
3 garlic cloves, crushed
1 green chilli, chopped
½ teaspoon Kashmiri
   chilli powder
½ teaspoon garam masala
   (see page 51)
½ teaspoon ground roasted
   cumin seeds
2 tomatoes, diced
2 tablespoons chopped
   coriander
squeeze of lime

Put the whole aubergines over two gas flames burning on a medium heat and roast them, turning frequently, until the skin is charred and the flesh has collapsed (about 12–15 minutes). Transfer to a roasting tray and leave to cool. Remove most of the skin with your fingers, leaving a few flecks on the aubergine to add extra flavour. Roughly mash the flesh with a fork and set aside.

Heat the ghee or butter in a frying pan over a medium-low heat. Add the onions and cook for 8–10 minutes, until browned. Add the ginger, garlic and chilli and allow to cook out for 1–2 minutes.

Stir in the chilli powder, garam masala, cumin and tomatoes and fry for a further 1 minute, then add the aubergine pulp and cook over a low heat for about 10 minutes, until the aubergine turns a russet brown. Stir in the coriander and finish with a squeeze of lime.

CRUSHED TAMARIND POTATOES

This sweet-and-sour bowl of potato goodness commands a prime position at the table. The magic starts with the sizzle of fenugreek and fennel seeds as they are dropped into ghee or oil, followed by a flurry of spice-box staples. It's a punchy mix, sharpened with softened tomatoes and tart tamarind, and provides a rousing setting for plainly boiled potatoes. Innocuous-looking beige fenugreek seeds don't have an aroma in their raw state, but once fried in ghee or oil, they release a celery-like flavour, which adds depth and a slightly pickled character to the dish.

The classic partner for these potatoes is puris (see page 151). *Puri alu* is most often made for Sunday lunches, but it also travels well and, in India, is a regular sight on picnics and long train journeys.

SERVES 4–6

Boil the potatoes in plenty of salted water until tender, then drain and roughly crush them with a fork while they are still hot.

Heat the ghee or oil in a medium pan over a medium heat and add the fenugreek seeds, then the fennel seeds and cook for about 30 seconds. Reduce the heat to low, then add the chillies powder and turmeric, then the tomatoes, chillies and sugar. Cook for a few more minutes until the tomatoes have softened.

Stir in the crushed potatoes and add enough tamarind pulp to sharpen. Place over a medium-low heat to heat through, then stir in the chopped coriander. Serve with puris.

750g floury potatoes, such as
   Maris Piper or King Edward,
   peeled and cut into chunks
   if large
50g ghee (see page 26)
   or 3–4 tablespoons
   sunflower oil
¼ teaspoon fenugreek seeds
2 teaspoons fennel seeds
½ teaspoon Kashmiri
   chilli powder
½ teaspoon ground turmeric
4 tomatoes, roughly chopped
2 green chillies, deseeded and
   finely chopped
2 teaspoons caster sugar
50g wet tamarind pulp, seedless
   (see page 158)
2 tablespoons chopped
   coriander
puris, to serve (see page 151)

ADRAK PHOOL GOBI
PUNJABI CAULIFLOWER WITH GINGER

This lovely recipe for *adrak phool gobi* – turmeric-hued cauliflower florets, flecked with cumin, ginger and red chilli – is a simple and comforting northern Indian classic. It's cooked in a similar way across Punjab, sometimes without the onion and ground coriander, and often with the addition of potatoes (see the variation in the box below). There's some dispute over the cooking time: the jury's out on whether these florets should have a bite to them, or if total tenderness is the way forward. Extra cooking time lends sweetness to the finished dish, but crisp florets will retain texture and astringency.

There's no denying that Punjabis love their *phool gobi*, the Hindi term meaning 'flowering cabbage'. It's a regular feature of weekday lunches, and often enjoyed alongside tarka dal (see page 85), hot chapatis (see page 148) and raita (see page 166).

SERVES 4

4–6 tablespoons sunflower oil
1½ teaspoons cumin seeds
¾ teaspoon dried red chilli flakes
50g root ginger, peeled and
    finely chopped
¾ teaspoon ground turmeric
1 teaspoon ground roasted
    coriander seeds
1 cauliflower, cut into small florets
    (about 800g)
1 red onion, thickly sliced

Heat the oil in a karahi or wok over a medium heat. Add the cumin seeds and chilli flakes and fry for about 30 seconds, until the cumin releases its nutty aroma.

Add the ginger and, after a few seconds, the turmeric followed by the coriander and cauliflower. Stir well to coat the florets in the spices, and cook, stirring occasionally, for about 10 minutes, until the cauliflower has started to soften.

Reduce the heat to low, cover with a lid and continue cooking for 10–15 minutes, stirring every few minutes, until the cauliflower is tender, but still has a slight bite. Remove the lid, add the sliced onion and continue cooking for about 5 minutes, until the onion has softened.

ALU GOBI

Peel and chop 2 floury potatoes, such as Maris Piper or King Edward, into 2cm chunks and add them to the karahi or wok along with the turmeric and ground coriander. Cover the pan and cook over a low heat until the potatoes are half-cooked (about 10 minutes), and then stir in the cauliflower florets and continue cooking according to the recipe.

METHI ALU
FRESH FENUGREEK POTATOES

Fresh fenugreek leaves, known as *methi*, have a bittersweet flavour and are often cooked with potatoes, kneaded into dough and simmered in dals. Unlike the pungent seeds and peppery dried leaves, *methi*'s astringency mellows as it softens in the pan. Stripping the leaves from the stalks is an exercise in mindfulness, but if you don't have helping hands to speed up the process, frozen *methi*, which is sold at most Indian grocery stores and many supermarkets, is a decent option. As there are no stalks in the frozen packet and the leaves are already softened, use a quarter of the quantity indicated for fresh leaves. This simple potato-fenugreek dish is packed into countless lunchtime tiffin boxes across northern India and often served with parathas (see page 149), thick yoghurt and a perky pickle on the side.

SERVES 4

Pick the leaves from the fenugreek leaves and discard the stems.

Heat the ghee or oil in a karahi or wok over a medium heat. Add the cumin seeds and dried chillies and fry for 30 seconds, or until the cumin releases its nutty aroma. Stir in the garlic, ginger and asafoetida (if using) and, after a few seconds, add the turmeric, cooked potatoes and green chilli.

Reduce the heat to low and gently fry the potatoes for 2–3 minutes, then add the fenugreek leaves and ground coriander and cumin. Cook for a further 5–7 minutes, stirring regularly, until the masala clings to the potatoes.

500g bunch fresh fenugreek (*methi*), washed and patted dry with kitchen paper
50g ghee (see page 26) or 3–4 tablespoons sunflower oil
1 teaspoon cumin seeds
2 dried Kashmiri chillies
4 garlic cloves, finely chopped
30g root ginger, peeled and finely chopped
¼ teaspoon ground asafoetida (*heeng*), optional
½ teaspoon ground turmeric
500g new potatoes, boiled and halved
1 green chilli, finely chopped
1 teaspoon ground roasted coriander seeds
1 teaspoon ground roasted cumin seeds

CARROT, LENTIL AND COCONUT PACHADI

Crunchy, colourful and refreshing, a Keralan *pachadi* sits somewhere between a salad, raita and side vegetable. Its base is made from creamy yoghurt, enriched with pounded coconut, but what gives it zing is a scattering of crunchy fried lentils, popped mustard seeds and crackling curry leaves. This dish contains grated carrots, but you could make other *pachadis* with the likes of crisp-fried okra, shredded cucumber, cooked pumpkin, and even chopped pineapple or mango.

Coconut is a core ingredient in southern Indian cooking, where cooks grind the flesh to a silken consistency on a grinding stone or with a mortar and pestle. Electric 'mixies' are slowly replacing these traditional techniques – and Indian machines can pulverise ingredients to a paste in seconds. Sadly, many Western domestic food processors struggle to get the consistency right, so I've used ready-prepared coconut cream for this dish.

SERVES 4

2 tablespoons coconut or
  sunflower oil
1 teaspoon black mustard seeds
¼ teaspoon fenugreek seeds
1 teaspoon skinned, white urad
  lentils (*dhuli urad dal*)
1 teaspoon split Bengal gram
  (*chana dal*)
2 red chillies, slit and deseeded
1 teaspoon cumin seeds
30g root ginger, peeled
  and grated
about 15 fresh curry leaves
3 tablespoons coconut cream
1 green chilli, deseeded and
  finely chopped
1 teaspoon jaggery or light
  brown soft sugar
500g carrots, grated
100g full-fat Greek yoghurt
1 tablespoon chopped coriander

Heat the oil in a karahi or wok over a medium heat. Add the mustard seeds and fry for a few seconds, then add the fenugreek seeds, both types of lentil, red chillies, cumin seeds and ginger, and stir for about 2–3 minutes, until the *urad dal* is golden. Add the curry leaves and fry for a further 30 seconds, until the leaves smell aromatic (but don't let them burn).

Stir in the coconut cream, green chilli and jaggery or sugar, followed by the carrots. Cook over a low heat for 5 minutes, then fold in the yoghurt and chopped coriander. Serve warm or chilled.

GUJARATI SWEET-AND-SOUR DAL

Exuberant spicing, tamarind tartness and butterscotch sweetness define a good Gujarati dal. This one starts off as a smooth purée of lentils and peanuts and is gradually layered up with contrasting flavours, and finished with a flamboyant tarka of fried spices, which include whole red chillies, cloves and citrussy curry leaves. Gujaratis routinely add jaggery to dals, which results in a sweet, sour and often fiery flavour.

This recipe uses *arhar dal*, also known as *toor dal* or split pigeon pea – they are easily digestible and cook down to a delicious, buttery smooth texture.

SERVES 4–6

Soak the split pigeon peas and peanuts in hot water for 1 hour, then drain. Discard the soaking water and transfer the split peas and peanuts to a pressure cooker or large pan. Add the ginger, turmeric and oil and pour over enough water to cover by about 4cm.

If using a pressure cooker, cook the split peas and peanuts for 20 minutes, until they are completely soft. Let the pressure release naturally from the cooker, then open its lid and leave to cool slightly. If using a regular pan, bring to a simmer over a low heat – the dal will take about 80–90 minutes to become tender and you may need to top up the water level as it simmers.

Transfer to a bowl and use a stick blender or liquidiser to blend the dal to a smooth purée. Rinse out the cooking pan and return the dal to it. Add the chillies, tamarind pulp, jaggery or sugar and tomato and simmer, uncovered, over a medium-low heat for 15 minutes, adding more water if needed. Aim for a thin, soupy consistency.

For the tempering, heat the ghee or oil in a small pan over a medium heat and add the mustard seeds, dried chillies, fenugreek, cumin, cloves and curry leaves. Fry the spices, stirring, for about 40 seconds, until they are aromatic, then add them to the dal. Sharpen with lime juice and finish with chopped coriander.

275g split pigeon peas (*toor dal*)
25g unsalted peanuts, skinned
35g root ginger, peeled and
    finely chopped
½ teaspoon ground turmeric
1 teaspoon sunflower oil
2 green chillies, deseeded and
    finely chopped
4 tablespoons wet tamarind pulp,
    seedless (see page 158)
50g jaggery or light brown
    soft sugar
1 large tomato, finely chopped
juice of 1 lime
2 tablespoons chopped
    coriander

FOR THE TEMPERING
40g ghee (see page 26) or
    3 tablespoons sunflower oil
1 teaspoon black mustard seeds
2 dried Kashmiri chillies
¼ teaspoon fenugreek seeds
1 teaspoon cumin seeds
4 cloves
about 30 fresh curry leaves

SEVEN TIPS FOR COOKING LENTILS, BEANS AND PULSES

- A pressure cooker is a cook's best friend – it saves hours of cooking time.

- Buy lentils and pulses in small quantities. If they have been sitting around in your cupboards for more than 6 months, they will take much longer to cook.

- Soaking lentils and pulses before cooking ensures that they will need less time on the stove.

- Some small-sized lentils, such as red lentils (*masoor dal*), yellow moong and skinned, white urad lentils (*dhuli urad dal*) don't need to be pre-soaked, but larger lentils such as split Bengal gram (*chana dal*) and pigeon peas (*arhar* or *toor*) benefit from being soaked for 1 hour before cooking. Whole black gram (*sabut urad*), whole green gram (*sabut moong*) and dried beans and pulses will need pre-soaking overnight.

- If you don't have time to soak lentils and pulses, cover them with water, bring them to the boil, then turn off the heat. Put a lid on the pan and set aside for 1 hour. This will be enough to slightly tenderise them and shorten the cooking time. Use as you would for pre-soaked lentils and pulses, and add the cooking liquor into the masala.

- When making a tarka (the finishing ingredients for dal), have all the ingredients prepared and within easy reach, because so much depends on adding spices at the right time. If the oil is too cold, the spices won't release their aromatic flavour – if it is too hot, they will scorch and impart a bitter taste to the dal.

- Adding salt to the water when cooking lentils, beans and pulses doesn't have a detrimental effect – it's a myth that salt toughens them.

FIVE TIPS FOR COOKING WITH YOGHURT

- Use full-fat, creamy Greek yoghurt rather than a low-fat variety because the higher fat content makes the yoghurt more stable when heated.

- Adding a little gram flour will help prevent the yoghurt from splitting while it is on the stove.

- Slacken thick yoghurt with a little milk if you prefer a thin raita.

- Use Greek yoghurt instead of cream for a lighter flavour in slow-cooked lentils with cream (see page 78), vegetable korma (see page 115) and paneer, peppers and spinach in makhani sauce (see page 107).

- Thick yoghurt, strained in muslin, is a good foundation for dips and fillings. Add crushed garlic, deseeded and finely chopped green chillies, chopped coriander and coarsely ground black peppercorns for a fresh-tasting dip. Saffron is added to strained yoghurt and used in an aromatic filling for bulgur wheat tikkis (see page 20).

BUTTERBEAN AND CASHEW MASALA

This party dish has a big Punjabi heart. Golden-fried onions are enriched with pounded cashew nuts, which have been blended with tomatoes, garlic and ginger. The idea of using nut paste is an old technique, favoured in Mughal palace kitchens. Besides imparting richness, the paste also thickens the sauce. You could make this curry with cubed paneer instead of using the beans and fenugreek leaves. If you use shop-bought paneer, remember to soak it in hot water before adding it to the pan just before serving.

SERVES 4

75g cashew nuts
seeds from 4 green
    cardamom pods
2 teaspoons caster sugar
6 cloves
4 garlic cloves, chopped
20g root ginger, peeled
    and chopped
1 x 400g can of chopped
    tomatoes

FOR THE MASALA

4–6 tablespoons sunflower oil
2 Indian bay leaves (*tej patta*)
    or 3cm cinnamon stick
2 onions, finely chopped
1 large bunch of fresh fenugreek
    (*methi*), enough for 125g
    picked leaves, washed and
    patted dry with kitchen paper
1 teaspoon Kashmiri
    chilli powder
1 teaspoon ground roasted
    coriander seeds
1 teaspoon ground roasted
    cumin seeds
2 green chillies, slit (stem intact)
1 x 400g can of butterbeans,
    drained and rinsed
2 teaspoons dried fenugreek
    leaves (*kasuri methi*)
1 tablespoon thick double cream

Set aside 25g of the cashew nuts. Place the remaining 50g in a medium pan, cover with hot water and leave to soak for 1 hour or longer.

Put the cardamom seeds and sugar in an electric grinder and grind to a powder. Add this mixture to the cashew nuts and soaking water, along with the cloves, garlic, ginger and chopped tomatoes.

Bring everything to the boil over a high heat, then reduce the heat and simmer, uncovered, for about 20 minutes, until well reduced and the nuts are softened. Cool slightly and then use a stick blender or food processor to blend the mixture to a smooth purée. Leave to one side.

To make the masala, heat the oil in a deep-sided frying pan over a medium heat. Fry the reserved 25g of cashew nuts for about 4 minutes, until golden, then remove from the pan and drain on kitchen paper.

Add the bay leaves and finely chopped onions to the same pan and fry for about 8–10 minutes, until golden. Stir in the fresh fenugreek leaves and cook for a further 2–3 minutes, until softened.

Add the tomato and cashew nut paste, chilli powder, ground coriander, cumin and green chillies. Bring the masala to a simmer, stir in the butterbeans and cook for a further 8–10 minutes, until the sauce has a coating consistency – add a little hot water if necessary.

While the beans are simmering, heat a small, sturdy pan over a medium heat and roast the dried fenugreek leaves for a few seconds. Tip them onto a plate and crumble to a powder and then add to the beans. Stir in the cream and scatter with the reserved fried cashew nuts.

CHANA ALU MASALA
CHICKPEA AND POTATO CURRY

It's widely acknowledged that this Punjabi classic, so beloved of the Sikh community, is one of northern India's most cherished dishes. Its onion-ginger-tomato masala makes a magnificent base for plump chickpeas and although there are many regional variations, everyone agrees that puffed fried breads and sharp-tasting relish are its natural partners.

The tartness comes from dried pomegranate seeds, which are sold as sticky seeds or ground powder. A word of caution here, the whole seeds are seriously challenging to grind and can impart a gritty texture. Ready-ground pomegranate makes life a lot easier, and still packs a punchy flavour. Use mango powder (*amchoor*) if you can't get hold of ground pomegranate. This dish benefits from being made a day or two in advance.

SERVES 4–6

First, make the relish. Combine the onion, chillies and ginger with the lime juice in a non-reactive bowl and leave to steep for at least 30 minutes, or while you make the masala.

Make the sauce. If you're using dried and soaked chickpeas, drain them and rinse under cold running water. Put them in a pressure cooker and cover with water by about 4cm. Cook under pressure for 30–40 minutes, until the chickpeas are completely tender, then remove from the heat and allow the pressure to release naturally. Then, mash some of the chickpeas against the sides of the pan.

Heat the ghee or oil in a medium flameproof casserole over a medium heat. Add the onion and fry for about 8–10 minutes, until golden. Stir in the ginger, potatoes, turmeric, garam masala and chilli powder. Fry for a further 30 seconds to cook the spices.

Add the tomatoes and cook the masala, stirring all the time, until it has thickened. This should take about 10 minutes.

Stir in the chickpeas and their cooking water. Or, if you're using canned chickpeas, add them to the pan along with about 300ml of extra water.

Simmer the masala for 10–15 minutes, adding more water if it becomes too thick. Stir in enough pomegranate or mango powder to give the curry a fruity and tart flavour. Remove from the heat. Serve with puris, with the relish spooned over.

150g chickpeas, soaked
    overnight in cold water with
    ¼ teaspoon bicarbonate
    of soda, or 1 x 400g can of
    chickpeas, drained and rinsed
50g ghee (see page 26) or
    3–4 tablespoons sunflower oil
1 large onion, diced
50g root ginger, peeled and
    finely chopped
150g new potatoes, halved
¾ teaspoon ground turmeric
¾ teaspoon garam masala
    (see page 51)
½ teaspoon Kashmiri
    chilli powder
1 x 400g can of chopped
    tomatoes
2 teaspoons pomegranate
    powder (*anardana*), or
    1½ teaspoons mango powder
    (*amchoor*)
puris (see page 151), to serve

FOR THE RELISH
1 small red onion, finely sliced
    into rings
2 green chillies, finely shredded
10g root ginger, grated
juice of 2 limes

MAKHANI DAL
SLOW-COOKED LENTILS WITH CREAM

This indulgent, butter-rich dal was originally a basic black gram dal made by Punjabis in Peshawar. It's widely acknowledged that the credit for *makhani dal* (as this recipe is known in India) belongs to Kundan Lal Gujral, the restaurateur who founded Old Delhi's Moti Mahal in 1947. Gujral's butter chicken was already a hit with local customers, but he was keen to find a star dish for vegetarians too. He added tomato, cream and butter to *kali dal*, and this is the result.

Make this dal at least a day before you intend to eat it, to allow the flavour to mellow. For a healthier, lighter version, swap the cream with Greek yoghurt.

SERVES 4–6

150g whole black gram
  (*sabut urad dal*)
25g split Bengal gram
  (*chana dal*)
25g dried kidney beans
1 garlic bulb, cloves separated
  and peeled
50g root ginger, peeled and
  roughly chopped
4 green chillies
200ml tomato passata
75g unsalted butter
125ml single cream
salt

Combine the black and Bengal gram and kidney beans in a bowl. Cover them with water and soak overnight, then discard the soaking water and transfer the lentils and beans to a pressure cooker or sturdy casserole.

Take a piece of muslin, about the size of a large handkerchief, and lay it flat on a work surface. Put the garlic and ginger in the centre of the muslin and make a bundle, securing the cloth with string. Add this muslin bag to the lentil mixture along with the green chillies.

Cover the mixed lentils and kidney beans with water by about 4cm. If you're using a pressure cooker, cook for about 30 minutes, then remove from the heat and allow the pressure to release naturally. Reduce the liquid over a medium heat until the lentils are thick and very tender (about 10 minutes). If using a casserole, simmer over a low heat for about 2–3 hours, until the liquid has reduced and the pulses are soft. (You'll need to replenish the water level from time to time.)

Using the back of a wooden spoon, lightly mash the pulses against the sides of the pan.

Squeeze any garlic and ginger juices from the bag into the dal, then discard the bag. Season with salt, to taste. Stir in the tomato passata, butter and cream and serve with Indian breads (see pages 148–154).

SAMBAR
TAMARIND AND VEGETABLE LENTILS

Across southern India, *sambar* and its many variations are as diverse as they are delicious. This is a hearty mixed vegetable and lentil stew, which can be enjoyed whatever the occasion – dunked with ginger and green chilli doughnuts (see page 24), as an obliging partner to lunchtime dosas, or as a mandatory dish at celebratory feasts.

Ready-made *sambar* powder is available in Indian grocery stores, and is handy for busy cooks, but it is worth making your own (see page 55). This full-flavoured blend of roasted and pounded lentils, chillies and warming ground spices promises to elevate your *sambar* to star status.

SERVES 4

First, snip the tops off the dried chillies and shake out the seeds. Set aside.

Put the washed split pigeon peas in a bowl and soak in hot water for 1 hour. Drain the soaking liquid and transfer the peas to a pressure cooker. Cover with water by about 4cm, add the turmeric and the 1 teaspoon of oil. Cook under pressure for 20 minutes, then remove from the heat and allow the pressure to release naturally. Alternatively, cook the split pigeon peas in a medium pan for about 45 minutes with the turmeric and oil, or until the split peas are soft and beginning to break up. Lightly mash some of split peas with a potato masher to break them up further.

Heat the remaining 4 tablespoons of oil in a large pan over a medium-low heat. Add the mustard seeds and deseeded dried chillies and fry for a few seconds, until the chillies darken. Stir in the fennel and cumin seeds and curry leaves, and cook for about 30 seconds, stirring all the time, until the spices are fragrant.

Add the onions, butternut squash, aubergine and carrot to the fried spices. Stir well and cook for 10 minutes, until the onions start to soften. Pour in enough boiling water to cover the vegetables, cover with a lid, reduce the heat and simmer for 15–20 minutes, until the vegetables are tender.

Add the chopped tomatoes and *sambar* powder, followed by the cooked lentils and enough tamarind pulp to sharpen. You might need to pour in a little hot water so that the lentils take on a soupy consistency, depending on how you like your dal. Simmer for 10 minutes to meld the flavours, then stir in the coriander before serving.

3 dried Kashmiri chillies
200g split pigeon peas (*toor dal*)
½ teaspoon ground turmeric
4 tablespoons sunflower oil, plus
    1 teaspoon extra
1 teaspoon black mustard seeds
1 teaspoon fennel seeds
½ teaspoon cumin seeds
about 15 fresh curry leaves
2 onions, sliced
150g peeled butternut squash,
    deseeded and cut into
    2cm cubes
1 aubergine, cut into 2cm cubes
1 carrot, thickly sliced
3 tomatoes, roughly chopped
1 tablespoon *sambar* powder
    (see page 55)
1–2 tablespoons wet tamarind
    pulp, seedless (see page 158)
2 tablespoons chopped
    coriander

LIME DAL

Drenched in lime juice and topped with a tangle of fried onions, this fluffy-textured dal is tinged pale yellow with turmeric and spiced with fried cinnamon, cloves, chilli, garlic and onion. Unlike soupy dals, this one absorbs its cooking liquid and has a distinctive, grainy appearance, earthy texture and lovely, nutty flavour. Skinned, white lentils (*dhuli urad dal*) have a mild, subtle flavour that makes them an obliging host for more strident ingredients. You could also use skinned yellow moong lentils for this dish – they'll probably need an extra 10 minutes cooking time.

SERVES 4

300g skinned, white urad lentils (*dhuli urad dal*)
1 teaspoon ground turmeric
50g ghee (see page 26) or
   3–4 tablespoons sunflower oil
½ teaspoon dried red chilli flakes
2 cloves
4cm cinnamon stick
1 teaspoon cumin seeds
1 Indian bay leaf (*tej patta*)
   or 2cm cinnamon stick
1 onion, diced
3 garlic cloves, sliced
1 teaspoon ground roasted coriander seeds
juice of 2 limes
2 tablespoons crisp-fried onions (see page 90)
1 tablespoon chopped coriander

Soak the lentils in hot water for 1 hour, then drain and rinse. Put the lentils in a medium, sturdy flameproof casserole and cover with boiling water by about 2cm. Add half the ground turmeric and simmer, partly covered, for about 20 minutes, until the lentils are tender but still hold their shape (you might need to add extra water as they cook) and most of the water has been absorbed.

Make a tarka. Heat the ghee or oil in a frying pan over a medium heat and add the chilli flakes, cloves, cinnamon stick, cumin seeds and bay leaf. Fry the spices over a medium heat for about 30 seconds, until fragrant, then add the onion and garlic and continue cooking until golden (about 8–10 minutes). Reduce the heat to low and stir in the ground coriander and remaining turmeric and fry for a further 1 minute.

Gently fold the tarka into the hot lentils. Cover the pan and set aside off the heat for 20 minutes for the flavours to infuse. Reheat the dal and sharpen to taste with plenty of lime juice, then scatter with crisp-fried onions and chopped coriander before serving.

TARKA DAL

Warming and comforting, this tarka dal takes its name from the way it is finished with sizzling spices, fried onions, ginger, garlic and chopped tomatoes. The recipe uses split Bengal gram (*chana dal*), a robustly flavoured lentil with a meaty umami flavour, and a favourite choice across northern India. You could swap the Bengal gram with split yellow peas, which are available in most supermarkets, if you prefer.

There's nothing pretentious about tarka dal – it's comforting and homely and seasoned with basic spices: turmeric, cumin seeds, chilli powder and aromatic garam masala. Fried ginger and garlic are a big part of its enduring appeal.

SERVES 4–6

Wash the Bengal gram, then place it in a bowl and cover with hot water. Leave it to soak for 1 hour. Discard the soaking liquid, put the gram in a pressure cooker and cover with water by about 4cm. Add the turmeric and oil and cook the gram under pressure for about 20 minutes, until the lentils are completely soft. Remove from the heat and allow the pressure to release naturally. If the lentils look too watery, cook for a few more minutes, without pressure – aim for the consistency of thick soup.

Alternatively, put the gram, turmeric and oil in a medium pan and cover with water by 2cm. Cook over a medium heat for about 1½ hours, until completely tender and broken down. Add extra water to prevent catching, as necessary.

Make a tarka. Heat the ghee or oil in a small frying pan over a medium-low heat. Add the cumin seeds and fry for about 30 seconds, until the seeds release a warm, spicy aroma. Add the sliced onion and fry for about 8–10 minutes, until golden.

Stir in the garlic, ginger and green chillies and continue cooking for a further 2 minutes. Add the chilli powder, garam masala and tomato wedges and fry for about a further 2–3 minutes, or until the tomatoes have started to soften. Tip this tarka into the hot gram and stir in the chopped coriander. Serve with Indian breads (see pages 148–154) or rice (see page 136).

200g split Bengal gram
   (*chana dal*)
½ teaspoon ground turmeric
1 teaspoon sunflower oil
50g ghee (see page 26) or
   3–4 tablespoons sunflower oil
1 teaspoon cumin seeds
1 onion, finely sliced
4 garlic cloves, finely chopped
30g root ginger, peeled and
   finely chopped
2 green chillies, shredded
¾ teaspoon Kashmiri
   chilli powder
½ teaspoon garam masala
   (see page 51)
1 large tomato, cut into 8 wedges
1 tablespoon chopped coriander

RAJMA
KIDNEY BEANS WITH TOMATOES AND GINGER

Rajma, as this dish is known, is to family dining in northern India what basic stews are to families in the West. This is the food we return home for, comforting food from Punjab's heartland. Deep maroon in colour, *rajma* is relatively restrained, favouring a light seasoning of cumin, coriander and warming garam masala. This simple dish is almost always served with rice.

Choose dark-coloured Kashmiri kidney beans, which are larger and fleshier than other varieties. The thought of pre-soaking beans might put off a few people, but it is worth it: the resulting texture and flavour are far superior to those of canned beans.

It's virtually impossible to dress up this dish – even chopped coriander feels like an imposition. All it needs is steamy rice, yoghurt, lime wedges, and (if you're feeling brave) a whole green chilli on the side.

SERVES 4

250g dried kidney beans,
   covered with water and
   soaked overnight
50g ghee (see page 26) or
   3–4 tablespoons sunflower oil
2 onions, diced
6 garlic cloves, halved
   lengthways
4 large tomatoes, chopped
2 teaspoons tomato purée
1 teaspoon ground roasted
   coriander seeds
½ teaspoon ground roasted
   cumin seeds
¾ teaspoon garam masala
   (see page 51)
½ teaspoon ground turmeric
1 teaspoon Kashmiri
   chilli powder
½ teaspoon coarsely ground
   black peppercorns
juice of 1 lime, plus extra wedges
   to serve

Drain the beans and rinse them under cold running water. Then, put them in a pressure cooker and cover with water by about 4cm. Cook under pressure for 30 minutes, until tender, then remove from the heat and allow the pressure to release naturally. If you're using a regular pan, simmer over a medium-low heat for 1¾–2 hours, topping up regularly with water as the pan starts to look dry. Once the beans are completely tender, mash some against the side of the pan into the cooking liquor.

Heat the ghee or oil in a large flameproof casserole over a medium-low heat. Add the onions and garlic and fry for about 8–10 minutes, until golden. Add the tomatoes and tomato purée and cook for about 5 minutes, until completely softened.

Stir in the coriander, cumin, garam masala, turmeric, chilli powder and black pepper. Cook the spices, stirring all the time, for 1–2 minutes, then add the cooked beans and enough of their cooking liquor to make a thick coating consistency. Simmer for 10 minutes, then sharpen with lime juice. Serve with extra lime wedges on the side, and boiled rice (see page 136).

GREEN GRAM DAL
WITH CRISP-FRIED ONIONS

Oval-shaped whole green gram (*sabut moong*) makes a musky and earthy-tasting dal – and when served with rice or bread it is a meal in itself. This is the kind of no-frills hearty offering served in roadside cafés across northern and central India. The tarka is reassuringly straightforward and calls for golden-fried onions, ginger and browned garlic, spiked with the sharpness of a split green chilli and a sprinkling of chilli powder.

This dal works well with rice or bread and makes a good partner for Punjabi cauliflower with ginger (see page 64) or fresh fenugreek potatoes (see page 67).

A pressure cooker is invaluable when cooking lentils and pulses. These sturdy pans are so much part of daily life that cooking time for dal is usually measured in whistles rather than minutes. There are at least 60 types of lentils and pulses used across India and it's easy to be overwhelmed by the variety. But dals are forgiving and open to interpretation – in fact most home cooks don't even bother with a specific recipe.

SERVES 4

Drain the soaked gram and rinse well under cold running water. Put the gram in a pressure cooker and cover with water by about 4cm. Cook under pressure for 30 minutes, then remove from the heat and allow the pressure to release naturally. Open the lid – the gram will now be fully cooked and should have broken down. If they are not quite ready, bring them to the boil and cook under pressure for a further 10 minutes, then let the pressure release naturally again. Alternatively, cook the gram in a medium, sturdy flameproof casserole, simmering over a gentle heat for about 1½–2 hours, until broken down – remember to top up the water during this time, as necessary.

Make a tarka. Heat the ghee or oil in a frying pan over a medium-low heat. Add the onions and fry for about 8–10 minutes, until browned. Add the ginger and garlic and continue cooking for a further 2 minutes, until fragrant. Stir in the chopped tomato, slit green chilli, turmeric, chilli powder and garam masala, and cook for about 3–5 minutes, until the tomatoes have softened.

Add the tarka to the hot gram, put the lid on the pressure cooker and leave the spices to steep for 15 minutes. Reheat the dal over a medium-low heat, finish with a squeeze of lime, and serve piping hot, topped with the crisp-fried onions.

150g whole green gram
(*sabut moong*), soaked for
1–2 hours in cold water
50g ghee (see page 26)
or 3–4 tablespoons
sunflower oil
2 onions, thinly sliced
30g root ginger, peeled and
finely chopped
4 garlic cloves, chopped
1 large tomato, chopped
1 green chilli, slit
½ teaspoon ground turmeric
½ teaspoon Kashmiri
chilli powder
½ teaspoon garam masala
(see page 51)
squeeze of lime
2 tablespoons crisp-fried onions
(see page 90)

CRISP-FRIED ONIONS AND BROWNED ONION PASTE

There's no better way to embellish a biryani or enliven daily dal than with a tangle of crisp-fried, salty onion slices. A handful of these onions, when blended to make browned onion paste, will enrich sauces with a nutty caramel-like flavour and also thicken creamy sauces. As little as 1 tablespoon of browned onion paste will enrich 350ml of sauce, but as with so many Indian dishes, there's no prescribed quantity and so much depends on personal preference.

MAKES 8 TABLESPOONS CRISP-FRIED ONIONS AND 4–5 TABLESPOONS BROWNED ONION PASTE

2 large onions, thinly sliced
fine salt, for sprinkling
sunflower oil, for deep-frying

Sprinkle the sliced onions generously with the fine salt, mix well and set aside for at least 1 hour. If you have the time, leave them for 3–4 hours to give the salt enough time to extract maximum moisture from the onions.

Using your hands (it's best to wear gloves for this), squeeze any water from the onions and then pat them dry with kitchen paper.

Fill a deep pan, karahi or wok half to two-thirds full with sunflower oil and heat to 180°C or until a cube of bread turns golden in 30 seconds. Deep-fry the onions in batches, until golden (about 3–4 minutes per batch), then remove with a slotted spoon and set aside to drain on kitchen paper. Once cool, store the onions in an airtight bag for up to 10 days; or make a big batch and freeze in a large ziplock bag.

For the browned onion paste
Put the crisp-fried onions in a food processor and add 4–6 tablespoons of hot water. Blend until smooth. Alternatively, put the onions in a bowl with the water and use a stick blender.

FOUR TIPS FOR USING BROWNED ONION PASTE

- A tablespoon of browned onion paste will thicken curry sauces for 6–8 people. In addition to enhancing a Mughal-style korma and biryani masala with its characteristic sweet-nutty flavour, this paste also enriches cooked dals and pulses.

- Because the paste is already fried, it's usually added just before any liquid or towards the end of cooking. It's also a good way to add extra flavour to Western dishes. A tablespoon of browned onion paste will enliven a vegetable stew for 4–6 people.

- Beat together 1 tablespoon of browned onion paste and ½ teaspoon of Kashmiri chilli powder with 150g softened, unsalted butter and use it on jacket potatoes, for coating roasted vegetables and for spreading over sourdough bread.

- Use browned onion paste in a yoghurt-based marinade for grilled paneer. Mix 1 tablespoon of onion paste with 4 tablespoons of full-fat Greek yoghurt, 4 crushed garlic cloves, 15g of finely grated ginger root and ½ teaspoon of garam masala. Add the juice of ½ lemon and 1 deseeded and finely chopped green chilli and coat this mixture over 240g of cubed homemade paneer (see page 104). Thread the cheese onto skewers and cook on one side under a hot grill for 3–4 minutes, then turn the sticks over and cook on the other side, until charred at the edges. Sprinkle the cheese with chaat masala (see page 52) and serve straightaway with lemon wedges on the side.

JACKFRUIT AND ORANGE BIRYANI

There are more than a hundred biryani varieties, each with their own distinct identity. This one, with its elegant spicing of citrussy cardamom, warming cloves and sweet cinnamon, features meaty jackfruit and fresh orange. Jackfruit is indigenous to South Asia and, as it is relatively bland, it is ideal for soaking up other flavours. Preparing fresh jackfruit needs muscle power, patience and a sharp blade. Alternatively, you can use canned jackfruit.

Show off this biryani with a simple raita (see page 166) and a mixed salad (see page 156). For added authenticity, try smoking the rice with charcoal (see page 120).

SERVES 6–8

350g basmati rice
1 teaspoon roasted and ground
   cumin seeds
1 teaspoon garam masala
   (see page 51)
1 teaspoon coarsely ground
   black peppercorns
½ teaspoon Kashmiri chilli
   powder
juice of 3 limes
1kg whole green jackfruit or
   1 x 400g can of unripe jackfruit
   in brine, drained and rinsed
500ml sunflower oil, for
   deep-frying

FOR THE MASALA
50g ghee (see page 26)
   or unsalted butter, plus
   1 tablespoon for finishing
6 green cardamom pods,
   pierced with the point of a knife
6 cloves
4cm cinnamon stick
4 Indian bay leaves (tej patta)
   or 3cm cinnamon stick
2 large onions, diced
50g root ginger, finely cut into
   very thin matchsticks
2 green chillies, deseeded and
   finely shredded
1 tablespoon browned onion
   paste (see page 90)

Put the rice in a sieve and rinse under cold running water until the water runs clear. Transfer to a mixing bowl and soak in cold water for at least 20 minutes.

Mix the cumin, garam masala, black pepper, chilli powder and lime juice in a large non-reactive mixing bowl.

If using fresh jackfruit, cut the fruit into wedges with a sharp knife, remove the hard, woody core and then the outer skin, and flick out any seeds. Whether using fresh or canned jackfruit, chop the flesh into 2cm chunks with an oiled knife. Mix the chopped jackfruit with the spiced lime juice.

For fresh jackfruit, heat the oil in a karahi or wok over a medium heat. Remove the jackfruit chunks from the marinade and deep-fry until golden. Remove from the pan with a slotted spoon and drain on kitchen paper. (There's no need to fry the marinated canned fruit.)

To make the masala, heat the ghee or butter in a sturdy, medium flameproof casserole and fry the cardamom, cloves, cinnamon and bay leaves for about 30 seconds over a medium-low heat. Add the diced onions and fry for about 8–10 minutes, until golden. Stir in the ginger and chillies and cook for a further 2 minutes, then add the browned onion paste.

Gradually stir in the yoghurt and then add the jackfruit (fried if fresh; or the drained, marinated canned fruit), followed by the orange zest and juice. Cover the casserole and simmer over a medium heat for about 30 minutes (or 10 minutes, if using canned fruit), until the jackfruit is tender. Add water if the sauce looks like it's drying out.

Meanwhile, heat the oven to 150°C/130°C fan/gas mark 2 and bring a large pan of salted water to the boil. Drain the soaked rice, add it to the pan, then boil, uncovered, over a medium heat for 2–3 minutes, until it's just a little less than half-cooked. Drain the rice in a colander and cover with a plate to keep warm.

Remove half the jackfruit masala from the casserole and set aside. Tip half the hot rice over the remaining masala, then scatter with half the mint leaves and half the crisp-fried onions. Repeat the process, using the remaining masala and rice, and cover the top with the remaining mint leaves and crisp-fried onions. Drizzle with the soaked saffron strands and water and dot the surface with the 1 tablespoon of ghee. Cover the casserole with wet baking parchment and a tight-fitting lid and bake for 45 minutes, until the rice is perfectly cooked. Gently fluff up the grains with a fork and serve straight from the pan.

150g full-fat Greek yoghurt
4 oranges, finely grated zest
    of 1 and juice of 4 (200ml)
handful of mint leaves
2 tablespoons crisp-fried onions
    (see page 90)
¼ teaspoon saffron strands,
    soaked in 2 tablespoons
    of warm water for 1 hour

WILD MUSHROOM PULAO

This fragrant pulao originates in the mountains of Kashmir and is notable for its smoky spicing, which makes a good match with the savoury, umami flavour of mushrooms and fragrant basmati rice. One of the key spices here is *shahi jeera*, or 'royal cumin'. A regular feature in Kashmiri cooking, it lends a distinctive, lightly smoked and astringent flavour to the finished pulao. Use regular cumin if you can't find this variety – it won't give quite the same flavour, but your pulao will still be impressive.

Although the original dish would be made with morel mushrooms, this recipe uses a mix of wild and cultivated varieties, and works well with regular chestnut mushrooms too.

SERVES 4–6

First, make the sauce. Whisk the yoghurt with the ginger, fennel, coriander, pepper, *shahi jeera* or cumin and crushed garlic. Set aside.

Dust the mushrooms with a brush to clean them, then thickly slice or quarter the large ones.

Heat the ghee or oil in a large pan over a medium heat and sizzle the black and green cardamom pods, cinnamon and cloves for 30 seconds, until they release their aroma. Add the onions and fry for about 8–10 minutes, until golden.

Gradually add the spiced yoghurt to the pan and cook until beads of oil appear around the sides of the pan. Stir in the mushrooms and slit chillies and cook for 2–3 minutes, stirring all the time.

Drain the rice, then gently stir it through the mushroom mixture. Add enough cold water to cover the grains by 1cm. Bring the water to the boil, then seal the pan with foil and a tight-fitting lid and cook over a gentle heat, until all the water has been absorbed and the rice is fluffy. Take the pan off the heat and leave the rice undisturbed for 10 minutes before gently fluffing up the grains with a fork. Serve with yoghurt or a raita (see page 166).

350g assorted wild mushrooms or a mixture of wild and chestnut mushrooms (stems removed, if necessary)
50g ghee (see page 26) or 3–4 tablespoons sunflower oil
2 black cardamom pods, pierced with a knife
6 green cardamom pods, pierced with a knife
5cm cinnamon stick
6 cloves
2 onions, finely sliced
2 green chillies, slit (stem intact) and mostly deseeded
350g basmati rice, rinsed and soaked in cold water for 30 minutes

FOR THE SAUCE
75g full-fat Greek yoghurt
1 teaspoon ground ginger
2 teaspoons ground roasted fennel seeds
2 teaspoons ground roasted coriander seeds
½ teaspoon coarsely ground black peppercorns
½ teaspoon *shahi jeera* or 1 teaspoon ground roasted cumin seeds
4 garlic cloves, crushed

LARGE
PLATES

SOUTHERN-STYLE MANGO CURRY

Mangoes are to India what strawberries are to Britain. Poems are written in their honour, regional mango competitions held in marquees and lavish mango festivals hosted in 5-star hotels. This curry originates from Kerala, where small, locally grown mangoes are simmered whole in spiced coconut milk. I've adapted the recipe for ripe mango wedges – their sweet flavour contrasts well with the bite of popped mustard seeds, crackling curry leaves, chillies and soothing coconut milk and yoghurt.

It's worth seeking out affordable southern Asian mangoes if you can – these are sold in shops from April through to September. South American mangoes are available all year round and, although they don't have such a defined flavour, the strident spicing in this sauce will carry them through.

SERVES 4–6

3–4 tablespoons coconut
   or sunflower oil
1 teaspoon black mustard seeds
1 teaspoon cumin seeds
about 15 fresh curry leaves
½ teaspoon dried red chilli flakes
25g root ginger, peeled
   and grated
¾ teaspoon ground turmeric
1 x 400ml can of full-fat coconut
   milk, whisked until smooth
3 green chillies, slit (stems intact)
   and mostly deseeded
250g full-fat Greek yoghurt
2 tablespoons coconut cream
2–3 ripe mangoes (about 800g),
   flesh cut into wedges
1 tablespoon chopped coriander
2 teaspoons curry leaf and
   coriander oil (see page 155),
   optional

Heat the coconut or sunflower oil in a karahi or wok over a medium heat. Add the mustard seeds and cook for a few seconds, then add the cumin seeds, curry leaves, chilli flakes and ginger.

Stir the spices for about 30 seconds, until they release their aroma. Then, add the turmeric and cook for another couple of seconds.

Reduce the heat to low and add the coconut milk and slit chillies. Bring to a simmer, stirring occasionally. Then, gradually whisk in the yoghurt and coconut cream, stirring all the time. When the sauce starts to bubble, turn off the heat and add the mango wedges and chopped coriander. Drizzle with curry leaf and coriander oil (if using) just before serving.

GINGER-SPICED PINEAPPLE AND TOMATO CURRY

This light and refreshing southern Indian curry is an antidote to the searing heat of Indian summers. Warm pineapple chunks and cherry tomatoes are cloaked in a coconut and ginger masala and seasoned with an astringent mix of mustard seeds, chillies and curry leaves. Coarse-textured *sambar* powder, with roasted ground lentils and fragrant spices, is sweetened with a hint of toffee-like jaggery, to provide an extra layer of sun-kissed flavour.

SERVES 4

Put the coconut, chilli and ginger into a food processor, cover with hot water, then blend to a smooth, slack paste. (You can use a stick blender, if you prefer.)

Heat the oil in a karahi or wok over a medium heat. Add the mustard seeds and fry for a few seconds, then stir in the curry leaves, then the onion. Fry for about 8–10 minutes, until the onion is golden.

Stir in the spiced coconut paste and continue cooking for about 5 minutes, until the water evaporates and the coconut darkens.

Stir in the *sambar* powder and cook for 1 minute, then add the jaggery or sugar and about 250ml of water. Cook, uncovered, for about 5 minutes, until the masala thickens to a coating consistency.

Stir in the pineapple and tomatoes and simmer for 1–2 minutes to meld the flavours. Serve straightaway with boiled rice (page 136).

- 50g frozen grated coconut, defrosted
- 1 green chilli, chopped with seeds
- 30g root ginger, peeled and chopped
- 6 tablespoons coconut or sunflower oil
- 1 teaspoon black mustard seeds
- about 15 fresh curry leaves
- 1 onion, finely chopped
- 1 tablespoon *sambar* powder (see page 55)
- 1 tablespoon jaggery or light brown soft sugar
- 300g fresh pineapple chunks
- 200g cherry tomatoes, halved

BAGHARE BAINGAN
AUBERGINES WITH PEANUT MASALA

This elegant dish has long been a jewel in India's crown. It reflects the refinement of Persian-inspired cooking techniques and incorporates punchy southern Indian ingredients, such as peanuts, tamarind, curry leaves and coconut.

Aubergines come in so many sizes, shapes and colours. This recipe calls for small, oval-shaped or round aubergines, available from Indian and specialist grocery shops. You could also use larger aubergines – just remember to allow extra cooking time. Choose firm, unblemished fruit, which feel heavy for their weight and yield slightly when pressed. They'll lose their looks during cooking, but the explosive, sweet-sour and astringent flavours of the masala will more than compensate. Roasted peanuts give texture, while coconut and jaggery provide sweetness, spiked with tamarind sharpness.

SERVES 4

1 onion, thickly sliced
75g unsalted peanuts, skinned
2 tablespoons desiccated
  coconut
1 teaspoon coriander seeds
2 teaspoons sesame seeds
1 teaspoon cumin seeds
1 teaspoon white poppy seeds
75g wet tamarind pulp, seedless
  (see page 158)
½ teaspoon ground turmeric
¾ teaspoon Kashmiri
  chilli powder
1 rounded teaspoon jaggery
  or light brown soft sugar
8 small, round or oval aubergines
  (about 600g)
4 tablespoons sunflower oil
about 15 fresh curry leaves

Heat a griddle or cast-iron frying pan over a medium heat. Add the onion and peanuts and dry-roast for about 3–4 minutes, until the nuts pick up flecks of colour. Reduce the heat to low and add the coconut, then the coriander, sesame, cumin and poppy seeds, and continue cooking for about 2–3 minutes, until the coconut darkens and the spices are aromatic.

Take the pan off the heat, transfer everything to a bowl and add the tamarind pulp, turmeric, chilli powder and jaggery or sugar. Stir to combine, then scrape the mixture into a food processor and blend to a thick paste, adding a splash of water if needed. (You can use a mortar and pestle for this if you don't have a food processor.)

Slit each aubergine from bottom to stem through the centre, but not quite all the way through – they should each hold together at the stem. Fill each aubergine with a dessertspoon of the spiced peanut paste, reserving the remaining paste to make a sauce.

Heat the oil in a large, sturdy frying pan over a medium heat. Add the filled aubergines and fry on both sides until the skin darkens and the flesh begins to soften. This should take about 5 minutes. Carefully transfer them from the pan onto a plate.

Add the curry leaves to the oil in the frying pan. Then, after a few seconds add the reserved peanut paste. Cook for 3–4 minutes, stirring all the time, then pour over 250ml of hot water or enough to cover the bottom of the pan.

Bring the masala to a simmer over a medium-low heat and return the aubergines to the pan, arranging them in a single layer. Cover the pan and cook the aubergines over a low heat for about 15–20 minutes, until tender and the masala has thickened (add a splash of water if it starts to catch on the bottom of the pan). Serve with Indian breads (see pages 148–154) or rice (see page 136).

PANEER
TECHNIQUE

Homemade paneer has a soft texture and bland flavour, which balances out the robust flavours of other ingredients in a dish. This is a fresh cheese, made by heating milk and curdling it with lemon or lime juice so that it splits into curds and whey. It's best to use milk that is close to its sell-by date, because it will be more acidic than fresh.

Commercially produced paneer is usually sold vacuum-packed in supermarkets and has a firmer, compressed texture than the homemade variety. If you're using a supermarket version, soak it in hot water for 10 minutes before using. This will make it more pliable. However, making your own is easy.

MAKES 240G

2 litres whole milk, close
   to its sell-by date
juice of 1 lemon
1 teaspoon fine salt

Put the milk in a pan over a low heat. Bring it to a simmer, stirring occasionally – this should take about 30 minutes.

Once the milk begins to bubble and rise up the pan, add 2 tablespoons of the lemon juice and the salt – the milk will quickly begin to separate. Add a further 1 tablespoon of lemon juice and continue simmering, until the mixture separates into curds and liquid whey (about 1 minute). The amount of lemon juice you need altogether will depend on the milk's freshness – the fresher the milk, the more juice you'll need for the liquid to separate.

Line a sieve with a double layer of muslin, then place it over a bowl. Pour the cheese mixture into the sieve and leave the whey to drain through the muslin or cloth. After about 10 minutes, draw the muslin or cloth around the paneer and gently squeeze out any excess liquid. Discard the whey.

Transfer the cloth-wrapped cheese to a tray and pat it out to a rough triangle about 2cm thick. Cover it with a tray and a couple of weighty tins and leave it for at least 2–3 hours in the fridge, or overnight, if you can. Unwrap the paneer. If you're not using it straightaway, submerge it in cold water and keep it in the fridge for up to about 3 days.

FOUR WAYS WITH PANEER

- Substitute paneer for eggs when making Punjabi-style scrambled eggs (see page 30). Add ½ teaspoon of ground turmeric to the onion and tomato masala, then fold in 240g crumbled or grated paneer. Take care not to overcook the cheese, otherwise it will become rubbery. This mixture also makes a splendid filling for samosas.

- For a tangy salad, soak 240g cubed homemade paneer in the juice of 2 limes, then season with 1 teaspoon of chaat masala (see page 52) and 1 chopped green chilli, with or without its seeds (depending on how fiery you like your salad). Add 1 tablespoon of chopped coriander before serving.

- To make a piquant paneer, stir herbs and spices into the fresh curds in the muslin-lined sieve. Chopped green chillies (with or without seeds, depending on preference), roasted ground cumin seeds, Kashmiri chilli powder and chopped coriander all make good additions. Wrap the cloth around the cheese and leave it to firm up in the fridge as you would for plain paneer.

- Traditionally, paneer features in full-flavoured masalas, such as peas with paneer (see page 108) and spinach with paneer (see page 142). However, it also makes great pakoras. A single quantity of the batter used for baby spinach pakoras (see page 15) will be sufficient for coating 240g of paneer cut into 1cm-thick rectangles.

PANEER, PEPPERS AND SPINACH
IN MAKHANI SAUCE

Makhani sauce – blitzed tomato, coriander leaf, ginger and lime, spiced with cumin and garam masala – is simple to make and provides a rich and indulgent base for soft, pillowy paneer. A little chilli reminds us that we're in India, and the addition of cream and butter reinforces the Punjabi credentials.

In India, milk, ghee, butter and cream are considered 'pure' foods and dishes made with them are served at celebratory occasions and auspicious events. Punjabis love to cook with dairy – so much so that cooks in rural communities will use their washing machines to churn butter from cream!

SERVES 4–6

Heat a dry, sturdy pan over a high heat. Add the spinach leaves and cook for about 1–2 minutes, until the leaves have wilted. Scoop them out, set aside on a plate and leave to cool.

Heat the oil in a karahi or wok over a medium-low heat. Add the onions and cook for 8–10 minutes until softened, then add the garlic and red peppers and continue cooking for 7–10 minutes, until the peppers have softened. Set aside.

If you are using shop-bought cheese, put the paneer in a heatproof bowl and pour over boiling water. Cover and set aside. (There is no need to soak homemade paneer.)

Make the sauce. Roast the fenugreek leaves in a small, dry frying pan over a low heat for a few seconds, stirring all the time, until aromatic. Tip the leaves onto a plate to prevent them scorching in the pan.

Put the passata in a liquidiser and add the roasted fenugreek, along with the ginger, sugar, green chilli, chilli powder, garam masala, cumin, coriander and lime juice. Process everything until smooth. (You can use a stick blender, if you prefer.)

Add the sauce to the onion and peppers in the karahi or wok and bring to a simmer. Cook, uncovered, for about 5 minutes, then stir in the cream. Once the sauce begins to bubble, stir in half the butter, then add the remainder when the first half has melted, stirring well between each addition. Add a splash of water if the sauce is too thick – aim for a coating consistency.

Drain the paneer from its soaking liquid and fold it into the sauce with the wilted spinach leaves just before serving.

handful of baby spinach leaves
3–4 tablespoons sunflower oil
2 red onions, thickly sliced
3 garlic cloves, very thinly sliced
2 red peppers, deseeded and cut into thick wedges
240g paneer (see page 104), cut into 3cm x 2cm x 1cm rectangles

FOR THE SAUCE
1 teaspoon dried fenugreek leaves (*kasuri methi*)
150ml tomato passata
20g root ginger, peeled and roughly chopped
2 teaspoons caster sugar
1 green chilli, chopped
½ teaspoon Kashmiri chilli powder
1 teaspoon garam masala (see page 51)
1 teaspoon ground roasted cumin seeds
handful of coriander
juice of ½ lime
125ml single cream
25g unsalted butter, at room temperature

MATTAR PANEER
PEAS AND PANEER

This wholesome dish, known as *mattar paneer*, is based on a simple onion-ginger-garlic masala cooked with softened tomatoes. Fried cumin seeds and aromatic garam masala shape the simple spicing.

It's not uncommon for groups of women in Punjab's rural villages to sit outdoors in the winter sunshine and collectively pod a huge heap of peas. It's as much a social activity as it is a practical pursuit. Sadly, time isn't always on our side and frozen peas, even in India, are a first port of call for busy cooks. It's worth making paneer from scratch for its superior flavour. However, if you're using the shop-bought variety, remember to soak it in hot water to soften its texture before frying.

SERVES 4

240g paneer (see page 104), cut into 2.5cm cubes
500ml sunflower oil, for deep-frying, plus 4 tablespoons
1 teaspoon cumin seeds
1 onion, finely sliced
4 garlic cloves, finely chopped
20g root ginger, peeled and finely chopped
¼ teaspoon ground turmeric
½ teaspoon Kashmiri chilli powder
½ teaspoon garam masala (see page 51)
4 tomatoes (about 300g), roughly chopped
1 teaspoon tomato purée
1 teaspoon caster sugar
250g fresh or frozen peas
2 tablespoons chopped coriander

If you are using shop-bought paneer, put the cubes in a heatproof bowl and cover with boiling water. Leave to soak for 10 minutes, then drain and pat dry with kitchen paper. (You don't need to soak homemade paneer.)

Heat the oil in a kahari or wok (the oil is ready for frying when it reaches 180°C on a food thermometer, or when a cube of bread dropped into the oil browns in 30 seconds), and deep-fry the paneer in batches over a medium heat for about 2–3 minutes, until golden brown. (Alternatively, deep-fry in a large, wide, sturdy pan no more than two-thirds full with oil.) Drain the paneer cubes on kitchen paper and set aside.

Heat the 4 tablespoons of oil in a separate karahi or wok over a medium heat. Add the cumin seeds and fry, stirring all the time, for about 30 seconds, until the seeds darken and release a nutty aroma.

Stir in the onion and cook for about 7–10 minutes, until golden. Reduce the heat slightly, add the garlic and ginger, and fry for a further 2–3 minutes, until the garlic and ginger turn golden. Stir in the turmeric, chilli powder and garam masala, then add the chopped tomatoes, tomato purée and sugar. Cook over a medium heat for about 3–5 minutes, until the tomatoes have softened, adding a little water if they catch on the bottom of the pan. Reduce the heat to low and simmer, uncovered, for 7–10 minutes, until the masala has thickened.

Pour in 100ml of water and, as soon as the masala starts bubbling, add the peas. Cook for 3–4 minutes, until the peas are tender. Stir in the cubed paneer and chopped coriander and serve with chapatis (see page 148).

KERALAN VEGETABLE STEW

This comforting dish is a favourite of the Syrian Christian community in Kerala, where it's fondly called *ishtew*. In the vein of many British stews, it doesn't have a list of prescribed ingredients, but that's where the similarity ends. Its seasoning includes ginger, cinnamon, cardamom, cloves and curry leaves, which make for a lively collective. The whole spices infuse the gingery coconut milk with a subtle flavour, which allows the vegetables to take centre stage. This stew is traditionally served with saucer-shaped pancakes known as appams, but it also works well with boiled rice.

SERVES 4

Heat the coconut or sunflower oil in a sturdy flameproof casserole over a medium heat. Add the cinnamon, cardamom and cloves and fry for about 30 seconds to release the aromas. Reduce the heat to very low and add the red onions, green chillies, ginger, curry leaves and black pepper. Cover the pan and continue cooking for about 8–10 minutes, until the onions have softened but not coloured.

Add the potatoes, carrots and Brussels sprouts, stir and then fry for 3–4 minutes. Put the lid on the casserole and continue cooking for a further 12–15 minutes, until the vegetables are tender. Check the vegetables from time to time, adding a splash of water if they look like they are catching.

Stir in the coconut milk and bring the sauce to a simmer, then add the coconut cream and broad beans and continue cooking for 2 minutes to cook the broad beans. Drizzle with the curry leaf and coriander oil (if using) and serve with rice (see page 136), semolina dosas (see page 124) or crusty bread. (Push any whole spices to the side of the plate as you eat the stew.)

4 tablespoons coconut or sunflower oil
5cm cinnamon stick
4 green cardamom pods, pierced with the point of a knife
6 cloves
2 red onions, thickly sliced
2 green chillies, slit (stems intact) and mostly deseeded
20g root ginger, peeled and thinly chopped
about 10 fresh curry leaves
¾ teaspoon coarsely ground black peppercorns
300g floury potatoes, such as Maris Piper or King Edward, peeled and cut into 3cm cubes
200g carrots, peeled, halved lengthways and cut into 2cm pieces
200g Brussels sprouts, halved
1 x 400ml can of full-fat coconut milk, whisked until smooth
2 tablespoons coconut cream
200g broad beans, blanched and podded
1 tablespoon curry leaf and coriander oil (see page 155), optional

CRISPY CAULIFLOWER
IN SAFFRON AND ALMOND SAUCE

This modern interpretation brings sophisticated, regal cooking and street food together on one plate. Turmeric-tinged cauliflower florets are marinated in garlicky chilli vinegar and then cloaked in a light gram-flour coating. Once fried, they make for a crunchy contrast to the creamy, saffron sauce enriched with pounded almonds and warming garam masala. Outside of Goan and Anglo-Indian kitchens, vinegar isn't often used in southern Asian cooking. Here, it imparts a lightly pickled flavour to the florets, which works well with this aromatic sauce.

For the sauce, you'll need to soak the almonds for 2 hours and the saffron strands for 1 hour before you can start cooking – so factor this into your timing.

SERVES 4

FOR THE SAUCE
50g almonds, blanched
pinch of saffron strands
2 onions, roughly chopped
75g ghee (see page 26) or
   5–6 tablespoons sunflower oil
1 tablespoon tomato purée
250g full-fat Greek yoghurt
100ml double cream
1 teaspoon ground roasted
   coriander seeds
1 teaspoon ground roasted
   fennel seeds
½ teaspoon Kashmiri
   chilli powder
½ teaspoon ground turmeric
½ teaspoon garam masala
   (see page 51)
2 teaspoons gram flour

FOR THE CRISPY CAULIFLOWER
1 teaspoon ground turmeric
juice of 2 limes
1 large cauliflower (about
   800g), cut into large florets
40g root ginger, peeled
   and roughly chopped
6 large garlic cloves,
   roughly chopped

First, make the sauce. Soak the blanched almonds in warm water for at least 2 hours. Bruise the saffron strands with the back of a teaspoon in a small bowl with 2 tablespoons of warm water. Leave for 1 hour or longer to extract the maximum auburn colour into the water. (The longer you soak the saffron, the deeper the water's colour and flavour.)

Drain the almonds, reserving the soaking water. Put them in a food processor and blend with 1 ladleful of the reserved water to a smooth paste. (You can do this in a bowl using a stick blender, if you prefer.) Spoon the paste into a separate bowl and set aside.

Add the onions to the same food processor or bowl and stick blender, and add enough fresh water to cover half. Blend the onions to a paste.

Heat the ghee or oil in a karahi or wok over a medium-low heat. Add the onions and fry for about 8–10 minutes, until golden. Stir in the almond paste and tomato purée and fry for a further 2–3 minutes, until the almond paste thickens. Leave the pan on a low heat.

Lightly whisk the yoghurt with the cream, ground coriander, ground fennel seeds, chilli powder, turmeric, garam masala and gram flour. Gradually add the spiced yoghurt to the pan, stirring all the time. Bring the sauce to a simmer and pour in enough hot water to give the sauce a coating consistency. Add the saffron and the soaking water, and a further 75ml of water, then set aside while you prepare the cauliflower.

Bring a large pan of salted water to the boil over a high heat and stir in the turmeric and lime juice. Add the cauliflower florets and blanch them for 5 minutes, then drain in a colander and pat dry with kitchen paper.

Ingredients and method continued on page 114...

1 teaspoon Kashmiri
     chilli powder
1 teaspoon ground roasted
     cumin seeds
1 teaspoon salt
75ml white wine vinegar
3 tablespoons gram flour, sifted
about 500ml sunflower oil,
     for deep-frying

Using a stick blender or small food processor, process the chopped ginger and garlic with the chilli powder, cumin, salt and vinegar until smooth. Using your hands (use gloves for this), coat the florets in the spiced, vinegary mixture.

Put the sifted gram flour into a large bowl, add the spicy florets, then turn to coat them in the flour.

Heat the oil in a karahi or wok (the oil is ready for frying when it reaches 180°C on a food thermometer, or when a cube of bread dropped into the oil browns in 30 seconds), and deep-fry the cauliflower florets in batches for about 5 minutes per batch, until golden and crisp. (Alternatively, deep-fry in a large, wide, sturdy pan no more than two-thirds full with oil.)

Use a slotted spoon to remove each batch from the oil and set the crispy florets aside to drain on kitchen paper.

Warm through the sauce and serve immediately with the cauliflower on top.

VEGETABLE KORMA

There is no definitive korma recipe, but everyone agrees that this is a sophisticated and richly aromatic dish, made famous by royal palace chefs. Traditionally, a korma is an onion-based braise where the main ingredient is cooked in creamy yoghurt that has been enriched with pounded nuts and aromatic spices, such as saffron – from the dried stamens of crocus flowers and one of the world's most expensive spices.

In this modern rendition of korma, the sauce is served separately from the vegetable topping. Edamame beans, although not traditional, provide a fresh-tasting crunchy texture, but you can vary the ingredients to suit your taste. This is a treat of a curry for a special occasion and far removed from bland-tasting versions so commonly seen in the West.

Bruise the saffron strands with the back of a teaspoon in a small bowl with 2 tablespoons of warm water. Leave for 1 hour or longer to extract the maximum auburn colour into the water. (The longer you soak the saffron, the deeper the water's colour and flavour.)

Meanwhile, make the shallot and nut paste. Bring a pan of water to the boil and add the blanched almonds and cashew nuts. Reduce the heat to low and simmer for 5 minutes, then turn off the heat, cover the pan and leave the nuts to steep for 1 hour. Put the nuts in a food processor with a little of the soaking water and blend to a paste. Add the shallots, ginger and garlic and process again until smooth. (You can use a stick blender, if you prefer.) Set aside.

Make the pounded spice mix. Using a mortar and pestle, grind the cardamom seeds to a powder with the mace, white peppercorns and sugar. Transfer the mixture to a small bowl and mix it with the chilli powder, ground coriander and garam masala. Set aside.

Once the saffron, paste and spice mix are ready, continue making the sauce. Heat the ghee or oil in a karahi or wok over a medium-low heat. Add the cloves, black cardamom and cinnamon stick and fry for 1 minute, to release their aromas. Add the shallot and nut paste and cook over a low heat for a further 10 minutes, until the shallots are softened without colouring.

Stir in the browned onion paste and the pounded spice mix. Pour in 400ml of hot water and simmer the sauce over a low heat for 10 minutes, stirring occasionally, until it thickens. Add more water if the sauce becomes too thick – aim for the consistency of double cream.

SERVES 6

FOR THE SAUCE
¼ teaspoon saffron strands
50g ghee (see page 26) or
   3–4 tablespoons sunflower oil
3 cloves
1 black cardamom pod, pierced
   with the point of a knife
4cm cinnamon stick
1 tablespoon browned onion
   paste (see page 90)
150ml single cream or
   4 tablespoons full-fat
   Greek yoghurt

FOR THE SHALLOT AND NUT PASTE
25g almonds, blanched in boiling
   water and skinned
25g cashew nuts
2 banana shallots, chopped
30g root ginger, peeled
   and chopped
3 large garlic cloves, chopped

FOR THE POUNDED SPICE MIX
seeds from 5 green
   cardamom pods
1 small blade of mace
¼ teaspoon white peppercorns

Ingredients and method continued on page 117...

Prepare the vegetables while the sauce is simmering. Bring a large pan of salted water to the boil and blanch the broccoli spears for about 1 minute. Then, add the green beans, followed by the edamame beans and the peas and continue cooking for a further 2–3 minutes, until everything is tender. Drain the vegetables in a colander.

Melt the butter in a karah or wok over a medium-low heat. Add the chopped green chilli and cook for 1 minute, then add the cooked vegetables and cook over a high heat for about 1 minute, until everything is warmed through.

Stir the cream or yoghurt and the saffron with its soaking water into the hot sauce and ladle it into serving bowls. Arrange a heap of green vegetables in the centre of each bowl, then scatter with crisp-fried onions and chopped coriander. Serve straightaway – you can remove the whole spices before serving, if you like; or serve traditionally with the spices still in the sauce.

½ teaspoon caster sugar
½ teaspoon Kashmiri
   chilli powder
1 teaspoon ground roasted
   coriander seeds
¼ teaspoon garam masala
   (see page 51)

FOR THE VEGETABLES
150g long-stem broccoli spears
125g fine green beans
125g shelled edamame beans
125g fresh or frozen peas
50g unsalted butter
1 green chilli, deseeded and
   finely chopped

TO SERVE
2 tablespoons crisp-fried onions
   (see page 90)
1 tablespoon chopped
   coriander leaves

SQUASH AND SWEET POTATO VINDALOO

Goa is the home of vindaloo, a masala which originates oceans away from the blistering-hot offerings sold in many UK curry houses. The Portuguese introduced garlic, chillies and wine vinegar (ingredients that provide the signature flavour) to Goa in the 16th century. In this version, the curry is warmed with cider vinegar and a palette of spices that includes black peppercorns, dried red chillies, sweet cinnamon and fragrant cardamom. Although vindaloo is traditionally made with pork, root vegetables are also obligingly helpful at soaking up flavour. Make it a day ahead if you can, to allow the flavours to mellow.

SERVES 4

1 small butternut squash (about 650g), peeled, deseeded and cut into 3cm cubes
1 large sweet potato (about 400g), peeled and cut into 3.5–4cm cubes
50g root ginger, peeled and roughly chopped
8 garlic cloves, roughly chopped
6 tablespoons sunflower oil
1 star anise
2 onions, finely chopped

FOR THE SPICE PASTE
6 dried Kashmiri chillies
1 teaspoon cumin seeds
1 teaspoon coriander seeds
½ teaspoon black peppercorns
¾ teaspoon black mustard seeds
¼ teaspoon fenugreek seeds
4 cloves
seeds from 4 green cardamom pods
4cm cinnamon stick
½ teaspoon ground turmeric
4 tablespoons cider vinegar
1 heaped teaspoon fine salt
3 teaspoons jaggery or light brown soft sugar

Make the spice paste. Snip the tops off the chillies and shake out most of the seeds. Heat a small griddle or sturdy frying pan over a medium heat. Add the seeded dried chillies, along with the cumin, coriander, peppercorns, mustard seeds, fenugreek seeds, cloves, cardamom seeds and cinnamon stick and dry-roast, stirring continuously to prevent scorching, for about 1 minute, until fragrant. Remove from the heat and set aside to cool.

Using a mortar and pestle or electric grinder, grind the cooled, toasted spices to a powder, then transfer them to a bowl and add the remaining ingredients.

Using your hands (it's best to wear gloves), mix the spice paste with the squash and sweet potato cubes to coat and set aside while you make the masala.

Using a food processor or stick blender, process the ginger and garlic with a generous splash of water until it resembles a paste. Heat the oven to 160°C/140°C fan/gas mark 2–3.

Heat the oil in a sturdy flameproof casserole over a medium-high heat and add the star anise. After about 30 seconds, stir in the onions and fry for about 5–7 minutes, until golden. Add the spice-coated vegetables and cook until the masala has browned – about 5 minutes. Add a little water if the spices catch on the bottom of the pan.

Stir in the ginger-and-garlic paste and cook for a further 5–7 minutes, until small beads of oil appear around the edges of the pan. Pour over enough hot water to half cover the vegetables. Cover the casserole and transfer the vindaloo to the oven for 1 hour, until the masala has thickened and the vegetables are tender. Serve with boiled rice (see page 136).

SMOKING FOOD WITH CHARCOAL
TECHNIQUE

Infusing dishes with delicately scented smoke is a centuries-old practice, famous in royal kitchens in and around Lucknow. It is most often used to impart an extra layer of flavour to rich biryanis, pulaos and kebabs. Its uses are varied and the resulting flavour is complex and richly aromatic.

4cm piece of lumpwood charcoal
3 tablespoons ghee (see page 26) or clarified butter
4 betel nut leaves or an 8–10cm square of strong foil

Heat the charcoal in a very hot oven or over a gas flame until it glows and takes on a greyish hue.

Warm the ghee or clarified butter in a small pan over a low heat.

While the ghee or butter is heating, either make a rough cup shape from the foil and lightly press it into the surface of whatever food you are smoking or overlap the betel nut leaves to create a rough cup shape and put them in the centre of the pan or dish containing the ingredients you want to smoke.

Using tongs, carefully transfer the hot charcoal to the leaves or foil. As soon as the ghee starts to smoke, quickly pour it over the hot charcoal in the leaves or foil. It will start to smoke straightaway – the aim is to trap the smoke and infuse the ingredients. Quickly cover the pan or dish containing the smoked food with foil and a tight-fitting lid and leave it on one side for 30 minutes. (If you are making a biryani or pulao, the pan or dish goes into the oven at 150°C/130°C fan/gas mark 2 for 45 minutes, instead of leaving it to one side for 30 minutes.) Remove the lid and discard the charcoal, the ghee or butter and the leaf or foil cup.

FIVE TIPS FOR SMOKING FOOD WITH CHARCOAL

- Take care when picking up hot charcoal and handling hot ghee: make sure that the tongs are made of metal and have a long handle.

- This technique works only with natural lumpwood charcoal – don't try it with briquettes because they have chemical additives.

- For extra aroma in the smoke, add whole spices to the leaf or foil cup. Any or all of the following would work well: a small stick of cinnamon, cloves, green and/or black cardamom pods, black peppercorns or a blade of mace.

- Always use extra thickness foil to ensure that it seals in the scented smoke without tearing.

- In India, chefs will seal the lid of the dish or pan, with the smoking food inside, using chapati dough so that no aromas escape. Sometimes, rather than using a lid at all, they will cover the pan with a sheet of pastry, which they then bake and eat alongside the contents. You could use puff pastry dough for this process. Or, you could seal the rim of the pan or dish to the lid with a stiff paste of flour and water.

TEN DISHES WORTH SMOKING

- Jackfruit and orange biryani (see page 92): pour hot ghee over the heated charcoal before the pan goes into the oven.

- Kashmiri chilli and cardamom potatoes (see page 49): smoke the potatoes before they go into the oven by pouring hot ghee over heated charcoal and then sealing the casserole with foil and a tight-fitting lid.

- Tandoori butternut squash (see page 123): smoke the spiced yoghurt with a 2cm lump of charcoal, before coating the butternut squash.

- Bulgur wheat and cardamom tikkis (see page 20): smoke the spiced wheat and lentil mixture before shaping it into patties.

- Lime dal (see page 82): smoke the lentils as soon as the dal is cooked.

- Wild mushroom pulao (see page 95): smoke the rice when the water comes to a simmer and then seal the pan with foil and a tight-fitting lid and cooked undisturbed until the rice is fluffy.

- Sweetcorn curry (see page 145): pour hot ghee over the heated charcoal after the curry is ready, before you add the topping. You may need to add extra milk if the curry thickens on standing.

- Plain yoghurt: put the yoghurt in a metallic bowl and smoke with the heated charcoal. Serve it plain or use it for a smoked raita.

- Mashed potato: pour hot ghee over the heated charcoal after you've mashed the potato with milk and butter.

- Rich tomato sauces for pasta: pour hot ghee over the heated charcoal after the sauce is ready.

TANDOORI BUTTERNUT SQUASH
WITH RED ONION RAITA

Marinated vegetables are the unsung heroes of northern Indian tandoori dishes. Although most of us don't have access to a clay oven, this recipe works well in a domestic oven turned to its hottest setting. Creamy yoghurt, sharpened with lime juice, garlic, chilli powder and zesty ginger, is contrasted with the sweetness of lightly charred butternut squash drizzled with honey.

Heat the oven to its hottest setting – about 240°C/220°C fan/gas mark 9.

Blend the onion in a food processor with the lime juice, chilli powder and oil until smooth. Use this mixture to evenly coat the butternut squash wedges. Line 2 roasting tins with parchment paper and arrange the coated slices over it in a single layer. Bake the squash for 10–15 minutes, until half-cooked.

Meanwhile, roast the fenugreek leaves in a dry pan over a medium-low heat for about 30 seconds, until aromatic. Tip the leaves onto a plate and crumble them with your fingers. Set aside.

Using a stick blender or food processor, blend the garlic, ginger, garam masala and yoghurt until smooth, then stir in the crumbled fenugreek leaves and divide in half. When the squash wedges are half-cooked, remove the trays from the oven and spoon one half of the spiced yoghurt evenly over the uppermost side of the squash slices.

Put the trays back in the oven. Cook the squash for a further 10 minutes then flip the wedges over and spread with the remaining yoghurt. Drizzle with the honey and continue cooking the squash for a further 10 minutes, or until the wedges are tender and the tops lightly caramelised.

While the squash are cooking, make the raita. Mix the garlic, sugar and cumin with the yoghurt and spoon it into a small bowl. Heat the oil in a small frying pan over a very low heat, add the chilli powder and warm it for a few seconds to release the aromatic flavour from the chilli, then drizzle it over the yoghurt.

Serve the tandoori squash with the raita, warm lime dal, and lime wedges on the side.

SERVES 4

1 red onion, chopped
juice of 2 limes, plus 1 lime cut into wedges to serve
1 teaspoon Kashmiri chilli powder
3 tablespoons sunflower oil
1 butternut squash, peeled and cut into 1cm wedges
2 teaspoons dried fenugreek leaves (*kasuri methi*)
5 garlic cloves, chopped
30g root ginger, peeled and chopped
½ teaspoon garam masala (see page 51)
250g full-fat Greek yoghurt
2 tablespoons clear honey
lime dal (see page 82), to serve

FOR THE RED ONION AND GARLIC RAITA
1 garlic clove, crushed
½ teaspoon caster sugar
½ teaspoon ground roasted cumin seeds
200g full-fat Greek yoghurt
1 tablespoon sunflower oil
½ teaspoon Kashmiri chilli powder

SEMOLINA DOSAS
WITH TAMARIND LENTILS AND COCONUT CHUTNEY

Dosas are pancakes usually made from a fermented rice and lentil batter. They're served with tamarind lentils, studded with vegetables (see page 81) across the southern Indian states of Kerala, Tamil Nadu, Karnataka and Andhra Pradesh. Perhaps no other staple has so many interpretations. This dosa is made with semolina, gram flour and cashew paste and enriched with coconut milk. Although softer in texture than rice-and-lentil dosas, its crêpe-like quality makes for a marvellous match with fresh coconut chutney.

SERVES 6

1 x 400ml can of full-fat
  coconut milk
150g fine semolina
125g cashew nuts, soaked
  overnight in hot water
pinch of ground
  asafoetida (*heeng*)
about 15 fresh curry leaves
2 tablespoons gram flour
½ teaspoon ground roasted
  cumin seeds
½ teaspoon coarsely ground
  black peppercorns
50g ghee (see page 26) or
  3–4 tablespoons sunflower oil
tamarind and vegetable lentils
  (see page 81), to serve

FOR THE COCONUT CHUTNEY
25g unsalted peanuts, skinned
25g coriander, chopped
25g root ginger, peeled
  and chopped
1 green chilli, deseeded
  and chopped
50g frozen grated coconut,
  defrosted
2 tablespoons coconut or
  sunflower oil
½ teaspoon black mustard seeds
¼ teaspoon skinned, white urad
  lentils (*dhuli urad dal*)
about 10 fresh curry leaves

Start the dosas. Pour the coconut milk into a bowl, then stir in the semolina. Cover the bowl and leave the mixture overnight at room temperature.

Make the chutney. Heat a griddle pan over a medium heat. Add the peanuts and dry-roast for about 2–3 minutes, until they pick up flecks of colour. Remove from the heat and set aside to cool.

Put the coriander in a food processor with the cooled peanuts, and the ginger, green chilli and about 200ml of hot water. Blend to a paste (you can use a stick blender, if you prefer). Gradually add the defrosted grated coconut and continue processing, adding more hot water if needed. Aim for the consistency of thick double cream. Transfer the mixture to a bowl and set aside.

Put the coconut or sunflower oil in a small pan over a medium-low heat. Add the mustard seeds and fry for 30 seconds, then add the lentils and curry leaves and continue cooking for a further 2 minutes, until the lentils have browned. Tip the contents of the pan into the bowl with the blended peanut mixture, stir to mix, then set aside for at least 15 minutes.

Meanwhile, continue with the dosas. Drain the cashew nuts from their soaking water and reserve the liquid. Put the nuts in a food processor and blend to a paste with a little of the soaking liquid, as necessary.

Mix the rested semolina and coconut milk mixture with the cashew paste. Stir in the ground asafoetida, curry leaves, gram flour, cumin and black pepper. The batter should be the consistency of single cream – whisk in a little of the reserved soaking water from the cashew nuts if it is too thick.

Heat a griddle or non-stick frying pan over a medium heat with 1 teaspoon of ghee or 2 teaspoons of oil. Pour a ladleful of batter into the centre of the pan and spread it out with a circular movement until it's 15–18cm in diameter and about 3mm thick (about the thickness of a £1 coin). Reduce the heat to low and cook the dosa for about 3 minutes, until it browns. Drizzle with more ghee or oil around the edges, flip it over, and continue cooking for a further 2 minutes, until golden. Repeat with the remaining batter until you have 12 dosas.

Serve the dosas straightaway with the coconut chutney and tamarind and vegetable lentils.

KOHLRABI BROTH

This Goan curry is based on a Portuguese potato, kale and chorizo broth, known as *caldo* or *caldhino*. I've seasoned this one with a mixture of lemony fresh turmeric, tamarind pulp and peppercorns, which I think complements the soothing base of coconut milk and vegetable stock.

Fresh turmeric will stain a bright orange, so wear gloves while handling it. A little goes a really long way – freeze any leftovers. Kohlrabi is not native to Goa, but provides a crisp contrast – you could use leafy greens, mangetout or courgettes instead.

First, make the spiced coconut milk. Blend all the ingredients in a liquidiser and set aside.

To make the broth, heat the oil in a karahi or wok over a medium heat. Add the onion and cook for about 5–7 minutes to soften. Add the garlic and, after 1 minute, stir in the chopped tomato. Cook for a further 3–4 minutes, until it has softened.

Add the kohlrabi and continue to cook over a medium heat for 5 minutes to allow it to absorb the flavours, then pour over the vegetable stock, and simmer, uncovered, for a further 15 minutes, until the kohlrabi is just tender, but still has bite. Add the green beans, cook for 1 minute, then add the peas. Pour in the spiced coconut milk and simmer for a further 5–6 minutes, or until the beans are tender. Aim for a broth-like consistency, adding hot water or extra stock if it looks too thick. Stir in the chopped coriander and serve as it is or with rice (see page 136).

SERVES 4

FOR THE SPICED COCONUT MILK
- 1 x 400ml can of full-fat coconut milk
- 1 teaspoon ground roasted coriander seeds
- 1 teaspoon ground roasted cumin seeds
- ½ teaspoon coarsely ground black peppercorns
- 20g turmeric root, peeled and roughly chopped
- 30g root ginger, peeled and roughly chopped
- 1 green chilli, chopped
- 2 teaspoons caster sugar
- 2 tablespoons wet tamarind pulp, seedless (see page 158)

FOR THE BROTH
- 3–4 tablespoons sunflower oil
- 2 onions, diced
- 2 large garlic cloves, finely chopped
- 1 large tomato, chopped with seeds
- 2 kohlrabi (about 500g), thick outer skin removed, then cut into 3cm cubes
- 500ml vegetable stock, plus extra to loosen if needed
- 100g green beans
- 75g fresh or frozen peas
- 1 tablespoon chopped coriander

PANEER AND POTATO KOFTAS
IN SPICED TOMATO MASALA

Koftas, which originated in the Middle East, are traditionally meat-based, but these ones are made with paneer. Flecked with dill and stuffed with apricots, they are fried and then added to a tomato sauce that has been spiced with the warming notes of garam masala and sweet cinnamon. It's important to use homemade paneer for the koftas as it has more moisture than shop-bought versions and holds its shape.

SERVES 4

2 tablespoons gram flour
1 floury potato (about 200g), such as Maris Piper or King Edward, peeled and quartered
200g homemade paneer (see page 104), coarsely grated
3 tablespoons chopped dill
4 tablespoons sunflower oil
1 large red onion, diced
30g root ginger, peeled and finely grated
1 green chilli, deseeded and finely chopped
50g soft, semi-dried apricots, finely chopped
2–3 tablespoons plain flour, for coating
500ml sunflower oil, for deep-frying

FOR THE MASALA
1 onion, roughly chopped
25g root ginger, peeled and roughly chopped
4–6 tablespoons sunflower oil
1 teaspoon cumin seeds
2 Indian bay leaves (*tej patta*) or 2cm cinnamon stick
½ teaspoon ground turmeric
½ teaspoon Kashmiri chilli powder
½ teaspoon garam masala (see page 51)
½ teaspoon ground cinnamon
2 teaspoons caster sugar

Place a small pan over a medium heat and add the gram flour, roasting it for about 1–2 minutes, stirring all the time, until it releases a toasted aroma. Tip on to a plate and set aside.

Bring a pan of salted water to the boil. Add the potato quarters and cook until tender. Drain them in a colander, then tip them back into the pan and mash with a fork. Stir through the grated paneer and chopped dill and set aside.

To make the koftas, heat the oil in a small frying pan over a medium heat. Add the red onion and grated ginger and cook for 5–7 minutes, until the onion is softened but not coloured. Add green chilli and cook for a further 1 minute. Transfer the mixture to the pan with the paneer and potato mixture. Add the toasted gram flour, stir to combine and leave to cool.

Shape the paneer mixture into 12 evenly sized portions. Using damp hands, pat each portion into a 5mm-thick disc on the palm of one hand. Put ¾ teaspoon of chopped apricots in the centre, then fold the edge of the disc over the fruit and shape into a small ball, about the size of a golf ball. Coat in flour, then set aside and repeat for the remaining paneer-mixture portions.

To deep-fry, fill a large, wide, sturdy pan no more than two-thirds full with oil. The oil is ready for frying when it reaches 180°C on a food thermometer, or when a cube of bread dropped into the oil browns in 30 seconds. Add the koftas in batches, frying each batch for about 3 minutes on each side, until they are golden all over. Drain each batch on kitchen paper while you fry the remainder, then set aside.

To make the masala, blend the onion and ginger in a food processor or with a stick blender, with a little water, until smooth.

Heat the oil in a sturdy frying pan over a medium heat. Add the cumin seeds, then after a few seconds, add the bay leaves or cinnamon stick and fry for 30 seconds, or until the cumin is fragrant. Stir in the onion and ginger paste and fry for about 10 minutes, until golden. Add the turmeric, chilli powder, garam masala, ground cinnamon and sugar. Cook for a further 1 minute, then add the passata and stock or water, turn the heat down and simmer, uncovered, for 10 minutes, until the masala thickens.

Add the koftas in a single layer to the pan and warm through, spooning over the sauce to coat. Drizzle with the beaten yoghurt and sprinkle with the ground cumin before serving.

200ml tomato passata
250ml vegetable stock or water

TO SERVE
1 tablespoon full-fat Greek
   yoghurt, lightly beaten
½ teaspoon ground roasted
   cumin seeds

TOMATO SALAD

This tomato salad, topped with fried, baby courgettes, boasts big flavours, led by fruity mango powder and tart chaat masala. It's a Mediterranean-style salad, dressed with olive oil and sherry vinegar, and spiked with Indian spices and plenty of herbs. Choose full-flavoured tomatoes for maximum impact, as the bland, watery varieties will let you down. Ready-made stock is fine for this recipe and provides a base for the spices.

SERVES 4

Put the vegetable stock in a pan over a medium heat with the coriander seeds, fennel seeds, garlic and chilli powder, and simmer for about 7–8 minutes, or until the liquid has reduced to 75ml. Strain the stock and leave it to cool until lukewarm. Whisk in the olive oil, sherry vinegar and sugar and then stir in the chopped herbs, shallot and diced tomatoes. Set aside.

To make the courgettes, mix the semolina with the mango powder, turmeric, chilli powder, chaat masala and 1 teaspoon of salt. Coat the courgette halves in the 2 tablespoons of sunflower oil followed by the spiced semolina.

Heat a 2cm depth of oil in a deep frying pan and fry the courgettes in batches until crisp on the outside and just tender when pierced with a knife – about 2 minutes per batch. Remove each batch with a slotted spoon, drain on kitchen paper and sprinkle lightly with sea salt.

Spoon the tomato salad onto a platter and pile the courgettes in the middle of it. Serve with the yoghurt and lime wedges on the side.

350ml vegetable stock
½ teaspoon coriander seeds
1 teaspoon fennel seeds
3 garlic cloves, thinly sliced
½ teaspoon Kashmiri
    chilli powder
2 tablespoons olive oil
1 tablespoon sherry vinegar
2 teaspoons caster sugar
1 tablespoon chopped dill
1 tablespoon chopped
    coriander leaves
1 tablespoon chopped
    mint leaves
1 shallot, finely diced
4 large tomatoes (about 400g),
    deseeded and diced
2 tablespoons full-fat Greek
    yoghurt, to serve
1 lime, cut into wedges, to serve

FOR THE CRISPY COURGETTES
2 tablespoons semolina
4 teaspoons mango powder
    (amchoor)
1 teaspoon ground turmeric
2 teaspoons Kashmiri
    chilli powder
1 teaspoon chaat masala
    (see page 52)
350g baby courgettes, split in
    half lengthways
2 tablespoons sunflower oil, plus
    extra for frying
sea salt flakes, for sprinkling

SPICED POTATO SCOTCH EGGS
WITH CASHEW NUT SAUCE

The origins of Scotch eggs are hotly contested. Some people believe they were inspired by an Indian *nargisi kofta*, a hard-boiled egg encased in spiced, minced meat and served in a curry. Others think of them as a British staple. This recipe pays homage to them both. Here, the potato is speckled with mustard seeds and seasoned with green chillies and *sambar* powder. It's then shaped around the egg and crumbed and fried until golden. These would make a lovely lunch with a crisp salad – but to stay closer to the tropical shores of southern India I suggest serving with a cashew nut sauce instead.

SERVES 6

6 eggs
4 tablespoons sunflower oil, plus about 500ml for deep-frying
1 teaspoon black mustard seeds
about 15 fresh curry leaves
2 onions, finely diced
30g root ginger, peeled and finely grated
2 green chillies, deseeded and finely chopped
1 tablespoon *sambar* powder (see page 55)
750g floury potatoes, such as King Edward or Maris Piper, peeled, boiled and mashed while hot
2 tablespoons chopped coriander
juice of 1 lime

FOR THE CASHEW NUT SAUCE
4–6 tablespoons coconut or sunflower oil
4 green cardamom pods, pierced with a knife
5cm cinnamon stick
1 large onion, finely diced
4 tomatoes, finely chopped
2 green chillies, deseeded and finely chopped
75g cashew nuts, soaked in hot water for 1 hour

Put the eggs in a pan, cover with cold water and bring to the boil. Turn off the heat, cover the pan and set aside for 8 minutes until hard-boiled. Shell the eggs and cover with cold water until needed.

Heat the 4 tablespoons of sunflower oil in a large pan over a medium-low heat. Add the mustard seeds and fry for 30 seconds until the spluttering stops, then add the curry leaves, onions and ginger. Continue frying for 8–10 minutes, until the onions are golden, then stir in the green chillies, *sambar* powder, mashed potato, coriander and enough of the lime juice to sharpen. Set aside to cool.

Divide the cooled potato mix into 6 equal portions. Using damp hands, flatten each portion into a disc measuring about 8cm in diameter. Dry the drained eggs on a piece of kitchen paper and put 1 egg in the centre of each disc, then shape the potato mixture around the eggs, making sure there are no gaps. Chill the coated eggs in the fridge.

To make the sauce, heat the coconut or sunflower oil in a karahi or wok over a medium heat. Add the cardamom pods and cinnamon and fry for 30 seconds, until they smell aromatic. Add the onion and continue frying for a further 8–10 minutes, until golden. Stir in the chopped tomatoes and green chillies and cook for about 5 minutes, stirring often, until the tomatoes soften and small droplets of oil bubble around the edges of the pan. Drain the cashew nuts, reserving the soaking water, and add the nuts to the pan with about 150ml of the soaking liquid. Simmer the sauce, uncovered, for 10–15 minutes, until the nuts are tender and the sauce has thickened.

Pour the whisked coconut milk into the cashew sauce and simmer for 3–4 minutes, until the sauce thickens. Stir in the coconut cream, then turn off the heat, cover the pan and keep warm.

To finish the eggs in the crumb coating, roll each potato-wrapped egg in the flour, then dip each in the beaten egg, then finally coat with the breadcrumbs. Fill a large, wide, sturdy pan no more than two-thirds full with the 500ml of oil. The oil is ready for frying when it reaches 180°C on a food thermometer, or when a cube of bread dropped into the oil browns in 30 seconds. Deep-fry the eggs in batches, for about 4 minutes per batch, until golden and crisp. Remove each batch with a slotted spoon and set aside to drain on kitchen paper.

Halve the Scotch eggs, arrange them on a platter and serve straightaway with the cashew nut sauce on the side.

1 x 400ml can of full-fat coconut milk, whisked until smooth
1 tablespoon coconut cream

FOR THE CRUMB COATING
6 tablespoons plain flour
2 eggs, lightly whisked with a pinch of salt
6–8 tablespoons panko or fresh breadcrumbs

AUBERGINES IN GARLICKY TOMATO MASALA

Softened onions, ginger, garlic and tomatoes make a marvellous foundation for fried aubergine chunks. However, it's the seasoning that gives this dish its distinctive character. Originating from the arid plains of Rajasthan in western India (where it is known as *achari baigan*), this recipe calls for a trio of pickling spices: sweet fennel seeds, bitter fenugreek seeds and astringent nigella, which punch far above their weight. It's a good idea to make this masala a day ahead, so that the flavours can mellow. As an alternative, try adding thickly sliced red or green peppers and courgettes to make an Indian-inspired ratatouille. Add them to the pan after the garlic and ginger paste and before the ground spices.

SERVES 4–6

Transfer the aubergines to a colander and sprinkle generously with fine salt. Leave on one side for 20 minutes to draw out the bitter juices, then rinse under cold running water and pat dry with kitchen paper.

Heat the 500ml of oil in a karahi or wok (the oil is ready for frying when it reaches 180°C on a food thermometer, or when a cube of bread dropped into the oil browns in 30 seconds), and deep-fry the aubergines in batches, until golden. (Alternatively, deep-fry in a large, wide, sturdy pan no more than two-thirds full with oil.) Drain the aubergines on kitchen paper and set aside.

Using a small food processor or stick blender, blitz together the ginger and garlic with enough hot water to cover and create a paste. Set aside.

Heat the 4–6 tablespoons of oil in a casserole over a medium heat. Add the fennel, nigella and fenugreek seeds and fry for about 30 seconds, until the fennel seeds begin to darken. Add the onions and fry for about 8–10 minutes, until browned.

Stir in the ginger and garlic paste and continue cooking until the water has evaporated – about 2 minutes. Reduce the heat to low, then add the ground coriander, turmeric and chilli powder and cook the spices for about 1 minute. Add the tomatoes and fried aubergine chunks and stir to combine.

Half cover the casserole and simmer the mixture, stirring occasionally, for 10–15 minutes, until the tomatoes have reduced to a thick masala, which coats the aubergines. Stir in the chopped coriander and serve warm or at room temperature with Indian breads (see pages 148–154).

3 aubergines (about 750g), cut into 4cm chunks, then chunks quartered

500ml sunflower oil, for deep-frying, plus 4–6 tablespoons

50g root ginger, peeled and roughly chopped

1 large garlic bulb, cloves separated, peeled and roughly chopped

2 teaspoons fennel seeds

½ teaspoon nigella seeds (*kalonji*)

¼ teaspoon fenugreek seeds

3 onions, sliced

1 teaspoon ground roasted coriander seeds

½ teaspoon ground turmeric

½ teaspoon Kashmiri chilli powder

1 x 400g can chopped tomatoes

1 tablespoon chopped coriander

fine salt

COOKING BASMATI RICE
ABSORPTION METHOD TECHNIQUE

Rice is central to southern India, just as bread is so important in northern states. There are many varieties of rice used across South Asia, and although each community has its own preference, it's generally agreed that basmati is top of the pile when it comes to aroma and flavour. Of course, this depends on its purpose – there's no point using the finest rice if it's going to be ground into a paste. Recipes in this book use basmati rice. Cooking rice by the absorption method retains its fragrance and flavour – we lose this if we boil it in water and drain the grains in a colander.

SERVES 4

300g basmati rice

Wash the rice in a sieve under cold running water until the water runs clear. Put it in a bowl, cover with water, and leave it to soak for 20–30 minutes.

Put the rice in a flameproof casserole and cover with fresh water by 2cm.

Place the casserole over a medium heat and bring the water to the boil. Then, turn the heat very low and cover the casserole with a tight-fitting lid. Simmer the rice for about 10 minutes, then lift the lid and check that the grains are tender and they have absorbed all the water. Add a little more water, if the rice needs it. Turn off the heat and leave the casserole undisturbed for 10 minutes.

FIVE TIPS WHEN COOKING RICE

- It's important to rinse rice under running water and then soak it for 20–30 minutes before cooking. This removes excess starch, which would otherwise make the grains clump together when cooked.

- Because the rice is usually served with highly seasoned dishes, there's generally no need to salt the water.

- If your pan doesn't have a tight-fitting lid, cover it with foil and then put the regular lid on. That way the steam that the water generates won't escape and the rice will cook evenly.

- Resist the urge to peek at the rice as it simmers – you'll lose valuable steam and the rice will take longer to cook.

- Gently fork the rice before serving, to fluff up the grains.

FIVE WAYS WITH BASMATI RICE

- For cumin rice, heat 3–4 tablespoons of sunflower oil in a casserole, then add 1 teaspoon of cumin seeds and let them sizzle for 1 minute. Add the soaked and drained rice and continue cooking by the absorption method. You can also use whole garam masala spices in the same way, to infuse the rice with a subtle flavour. Try it with the following: 2 black cardamom pods, pierced; 4 green cardamom pods, pierced; 4 fresh Indian bay leaves; 6 cloves; 4cm cinnamon stick; ½ teaspoon of *shahi jeera* or regular cumin seeds.

- A pinch of saffron strands, soaked in 2 tablespoons of warm water for 1–2 hours, will give the rice a lovely pale orange colour and also impart a sweet fragrance. Add the saffron and its soaking liquid to the rice as it comes up to a simmer.

- If you don't have saffron, and want a yellow colour and slightly astringent flavour, warm ½ teaspoon of ground turmeric in 2 tablespoons of sunflower oil, then add the soaked and drained rice and gently stir the grains to coat them in the oil. Pour over the water for cooking and cook using the absorption method.

- For a spicy kick, add 3 split green chillies to the cooking water.

- For lemon rice, heat 3–4 tablespoons of sunflower oil and add 1 teaspoon of mustard seeds, followed, after a few seconds, by 1 tablespoon of fresh curry leaves (about 15) and 20g finely grated root ginger. You could also add 1 teaspoon of skinned, white urad lentils for a crunchy texture. Stir-fry everything for about 1 minute and then stir in ½ teaspoon of ground turmeric and after a few seconds the juice of 1 lemon. Pour this mixture over hot, cooked rice and gently fold in.

SOUTH INDIAN RICE AND LENTIL PULAO
WITH EGG CURRY

This rice and lentil blend, known as *khichdi*, has many regional variations. Punjabis often serve it as a plainly cooked soup, spiced with fried cumin seeds; Bengalis elevate it to a celebratory centrepiece, seasoned with spices and studded with vegetables. This recipe, though, is from the south of India. The rice and lentils remain separate and fluffy after cooking and are spiced with ginger and Indian bay leaves. The accompanying egg curry provides plenty of tart, sweet-and-sour flavours. You could leave out the eggs, if you prefer.

SERVES 4

200g basmati rice
100g red lentils (*masoor dal*)
6 tablespoons sunflower oil
1 teaspoon cumin seeds
2 onions, finely sliced
25g root ginger, peeled and
    finely chopped
4 Indian bay leaves (*tej patta*)
    or 4cm cinnamon stick
125g frozen green
    peas, blanched

FOR THE EGG CURRY
4 tablespoons sunflower oil
¾ teaspoon black mustard seeds
about 15 fresh curry leaves
½ teaspoon dried red chilli flakes
2 red onions, diced
25g root ginger, peeled and
    finely chopped
½ teaspoon ground turmeric
1 x 400g can of chopped
    tomatoes
2 green chillies, slit
    and deseeded
2 teaspoons caster sugar, plus
    extra to taste if needed
1–2 tablespoons wet tamarind
    pulp, seedless (see page 158)
2 tablespoons chopped
    coriander
4 hard-boiled eggs, shelled
    and halved

First, make the curry. Heat the oil in a medium pan over a medium heat. Add the mustard seeds and fry for 30 seconds, then add the curry leaves and chilli flakes. Once the leaves stop spluttering (about 20 seconds), reduce the heat and add the onions and ginger. Fry for about 10 minutes, until the onions have softened but not coloured.

Stir in the turmeric and, after a few seconds, add the tomatoes, green chillies and sugar. Simmer, uncovered, for 10–15 minutes, until thickened. Stir in enough tamarind pulp to provide a slight tartness to the sauce (you might need to add more sugar to taste). Remove from the heat and set aside.

To make the lentil pulao, mix the rice and lentils in a bowl, cover with cold water and leave to soak for 15 minutes.

Meanwhile, heat the oil in a sturdy flameproof casserole over a medium heat. Add the cumin seeds and fry for about 30 seconds, until the seeds are aromatic. Add the onions, ginger and bay leaves and continue cooking for 10 minutes, until the onions have softened but not coloured. Drain the rice and lentils and add them to the pan.

Gently mix everything together and then pour over enough cold water to cover the grains by 3cm. Put the lid on the casserole and cook the pulao over a low heat for about 10–12 minutes, until the rice and lentils are tender and the cooking liquid has been absorbed. Set aside with the lid on for 10 minutes, then remove the lid, add the peas and use a fork to gently mix them through (the heat in the pan will warm them).

Reheat the curry sauce, stir in the chopped coriander and add the hard-boiled eggs. Serve with the rice and lentils.

RED CHILLI-STUFFED MUSHROOMS

The caps of portobello mushrooms are brilliant for absorbing and softening the potency of pounded red chillies spiked with ginger and lime juice. The pungent paste soaks into the mushrooms as they cook, and adds an extra kick of flavour to the crisp breadcrumb and gunpowder spice topping.

In southern India, gunpowder spice is a condiment, but it's also great for emboldening masalas, and here it is a key ingredient. Wilted spinach leaves finished with cream, softened garlic and just a touch of chilli flakes provides a flavoursome flourish.

SERVES 4

Heat the oven to 200°C/180°C fan/gas mark 6. Snap the stems from the mushroom caps and chop them along with the soaked and drained chillies. Heat the 2 teaspoons of ghee or butter and fry the chopped stem and chilli mixture with the ginger and black pepper for 2–3 minutes, until fragrant. Sharpen with the squeeze of lime and set aside.

Heat the 25g ghee or butter in a large ovenproof frying pan and fry the mushroom caps for 2 minutes on each side, until they colour and soften a little. Spread the stem and chilli mixture equally over the gills of the mushroom caps.

Mix together the breadcrumbs and gunpowder spice and pile it equally over the mushrooms. Drizzle with some of the ghee or butter from the frying pan and transfer the pan to the oven for 10 minutes, until the crumbs are crisp.

While the mushrooms are in the oven, make the sauce. Wilt the spinach leaves over a high heat in a large, dry and sturdy pan, then set aside.

In a separate pan, melt the ghee or butter over a very low heat. Add the garlic and chilli flakes and cook for 3–5 minutes, taking care not to brown the garlic. Increase the heat and add the wilted spinach, followed by the cream. Once the mixture starts bubbling, remove it from the heat and divide it between 4 bowls. Top each one with a baked mushroom.

4 portobello mushrooms
2 dried Kashmiri chillies, deseeded and soaked in hot water for 1 hour
25g ghee (see page 26) or unsalted butter, plus 2 teaspoons for frying
10g root ginger, peeled and finely grated
½ teaspoon coarsely ground black peppercorns
squeeze of lime
2 tablespoons fresh breadcrumbs
1 tablespoon gunpowder spice (see page 53)

FOR THE SAUCE
160g baby spinach leaves
1 teaspoon ghee (see page 26) or unsalted butter
1 large garlic clove, thinly sliced
½ teaspoon dried red chilli flakes
150ml single cream

PALAK PANEER
SPINACH WITH PANEER

Gingery-garlicky spinach, studded with soft rectangles of paneer, *palak paneer* is
§a regular feature in Punjabi homes and is usually enjoyed with hot chapatis (see page
148). Sizzling cumin lends a nutty flavour, while fragrant garam masala brings warming,
peppery notes. This dish is sometimes known as *saag paneer*, which is confusing. In India,
saag is a mixture of leafy greens, which includes spinach, fresh fenugreek leaves and other
lesser-known varieties. *Saag* is usually slow-cooked and retains a hint of bitterness, while
palak has a milder flavour and refers only to spinach leaves.

SERVES 4–6

250g paneer (see page 104),
    cut into 3cm x 2cm x 1cm
    rectangles
200g baby spinach leaves
3–4 tablespoons sunflower oil
1 teaspoon cumin seeds
4 Indian bay leaves (*tej patta*)
    or 4cm cinnamon stick
1 onion, diced
50g root ginger, peeled and
    finely grated
4 garlic cloves, finely chopped
2 tomatoes, roughly chopped
¼ teaspoon ground turmeric
½ teaspoon Kashmiri
    chilli powder
pinch of ground asafoetida
    (*heeng*), optional
½ teaspoon garam masala
    (see page 51)

If you are using shop-bought paneer, put the rectangles of cheese
in a heatproof bowl and cover with boiling water. Leave to soak for
10 minutes to soften the texture, then drain and pat dry with kitchen
paper and set aside. (You don't need to soak homemade paneer.)

Place a sturdy pan over a high heat, add the spinach and cook
for 1–2 minutes, to wilt, then transfer the softened leaves to a food
processor and blend with a little boiling water until smooth. (You
can use a stick blender, if you prefer.)

Heat the oil in a karahi or wok over a medium heat and add the cumin
seeds. Fry for about 30 seconds, until fragrant, then add the bay leaves
or cinnamon, followed by the onion, and continue cooking for about
8–10 minutes, until the onion is golden. Stir in the ginger and garlic and
fry for a further 1–2 minutes to cook out.

Add the tomatoes and soften them over a medium heat for 3–5 minutes,
then stir in the remaining spices.

Stir in the spinach paste and warm through for 1–2 minutes, then add the
paneer cubes. The heat of the masala will warm the cheese. Serve with
Indian breads (see pages 148–154).

PALAK ALU
Follow the main recipe, adding 300g halved new
potatoes to the pan with the ginger and garlic. Cook
the potatoes, with the lid on, until tender, then add the
tomatoes, followed by the spices and spinach paste.

BHUTTA KA KEES
SWEETCORN CURRY

Madhya Pradesh, a large state in central India, has a centuries-old culinary heritage and is home to this popular street food dish, known locally as *bhutta ka kees*. Traditionally, the recipe is corn-on-the-cob cooked in creamy spiced milk. Here, however, grated corn is mixed with spices, including ginger, nutty-tasting roasted cumin and green chillies, then added to a softened onion masala and simmered in milk. Chargrilling a couple of the cobs lends a smoky note to the finished dish, and its chaat masala and lime juice coating recreates the aromas of corn cobs being roasted over charcoal by street vendors.

SERVES 4

Heat a griddle pan over a high heat and chargrill both whole corn cobs for about 10 minutes, turning them frequently, so that all sides pick up colour. Remove them from the heat when most of the kernels have darkened and then use a sharp knife to shave the corn off the cob in clumps. Set aside.

Mix the grated corn with the garlic, ginger, cumin, green chillies, turmeric and sugar.

Heat the ghee or oil in a flameproof casserole over a medium heat. Add the asafoetida, followed by the onions. Fry for about 8–10 minutes, until the onions have browned, then add the grated corn mixture and the milk.

Cook over a low heat, stirring regularly, for about 5 minutes, until beads of oil appear around the sides of the pan. Add more milk if the corn masala becomes too thick – aim for a coating consistency. Divide the curry between 4 serving bowls.

Mix the shaved, chargrilled corn with the chaat masala and chopped coriander, then scatter the mixture over the curry. Serve with lime wedges on the side.

5 corn-on-the-cobs, 2 left whole and 3 coarsely grated
4 garlic cloves, crushed
20g root ginger, peeled and finely grated
1 teaspoon roasted and ground cumin seeds
2 green chillies, deseeded and finely chopped
½ teaspoon ground turmeric
1 teaspoon caster sugar
50g ghee (see page 26) or 3–4 tablespoons sunflower oil
pinch of ground asafoetida (*heeng*)
3 onions, sliced
250ml whole milk, plus extra to loosen if needed
1 tablespoon chaat masala (see page 52)
1 tablespoon chopped coriander
1 lime, cut into wedges, to serve

BREADS
AND
RELISHES

CHAPATIS

Chapatis are the mainstay of home-cooked meals across northern India. They're usually cooked on a curved, cast-iron griddle known as a tawa. Restaurants and roadside cafés will offer tandoori chapatis, known as *rotis*, which are cooked in a clay oven and are thicker, larger and more filling than the ones made in most home kitchens.

Most Indian cooks use gas hobs to puff up their chapatis. However, if you have an electric or induction hob, you can still make a good bread – it will just be slightly denser.

MAKES 12

250g chapati flour (*chapati atta*), or 125g wholemeal flour and 125g plain flour, plus extra for dusting and rolling
1 teaspoon sunflower oil
½ teaspoon salt

Mix the flour, oil and salt in a mixing bowl. Gradually add enough cold water (about 120ml) to make a firm dough. Turn out the dough onto a floured surface and knead well for about 7–10 minutes, until smooth. Return the dough to a clean, dry bowl, cover with an upturned plate or cloth and leave to rest for 30 minutes.

Add a little more chapati or plain flour if the dough looks sticky and then divide it into 12 evenly sized balls. Sprinkle each one with flour.

Heat a griddle until medium–hot. Put 3 tablespoons of flour in a small bowl. Using the palms of your hands, flatten one of the dough balls into a circular disc and dip both sides in the flour. Now roll it into a circle until it measures about 2.5mm thick and 12–14cm in diameter.

Slap the dough onto the hot griddle and cook for 1 minute, or until small air pockets start to form on its surface. Turn the chapati over with your fingers (take care) or with a palette knife or tongs and continue cooking for about a further 90 seconds, until the chapati picks up flecks of colour.

Gently press the bread with a clean cloth as it cooks on the griddle – the chapati should swell up with hot air. Keep turning the bread as it cooks.

Serve the chapatis straightaway or keep them warm in a cloth or wrapped in foil.

MOOLI PARATHAS
WHITE RADISH PARATHAS

Punjabi parathas glisten with ghee, and are a lot more indulgent than everyday chapatis. Enjoy these stuffed versions with plain yoghurt and a smidgeon of pickle on the side. Fillings are varied – here, I've used spiced white radish (also known as *daikon* or *mooli*), but cauliflower, spiced potato or chilli-speckled red onions are all popular alternatives.

MAKES 8 OR 9

First, make the dough. Put the chapati flour in a bowl with the teaspoon of salt, then sift in the plain flour and make a well in the centre. Pour in enough cold water to make a firm dough. Knead it in the bowl until smooth, then cover and set aside for 30 minutes to rest.

Meanwhile, make the filling. Put the grated radish in a colander and sprinkle generously with fine salt, then set aside for 15 minutes. Using your hands, squeeze out any excess liquid from the radish and transfer it to a clean bowl.

Stir in the carom seeds or garam masala, green chillies, ginger, chilli powder, chaat masala and chopped coriander until fully combined.

Divide the dough equally into 16–18 portions and shape each one into a ball, about the size of a table-tennis ball. Flatten one of the balls into a 4cm disc and dip each side in chapati flour.

Roll the ball into a circle about 3mm thick (about the thickness of a £1 coin) and 15cm in diameter. Spread a portion of the spiced radish filling over the circle in a 5mm layer, leaving a 5mm border around the edge. Moisten the edges of the dough circle with water.

Roll a second portion of dough as before and use it to cover the filling, pressing down well to seal the edges together.

Heat a griddle pan over a medium heat until hot, then drizzle with 1 teaspoon of ghee or oil. Carefully, lift the paratha onto the hot griddle and cook on one side for 2–3 minutes, until it begins to colour. Using a fish slice, flip over the paratha, drizzle 1–2 teaspoons of ghee or oil around the edges and cook for a further 2–3 minutes, until golden. Lift it on to a plate and serve straightaway with yoghurt and pickles. Repeat with the remaining dough balls and filling.

FOR THE DOUGH
250g chapati flour (*chapati atta*), or 125g wholemeal flour and 125g plain flour, plus extra for rolling
1 teaspoon salt, plus extra for salting the radish
250g plain flour
50g ghee (see page 26), melted, or 3–4 tablespoons sunflower oil

FOR THE FILLING
1 white radish (500g), peeled and coarsely grated
½ teaspoon carom seeds (*ajwain*) or garam masala (see page 51)
2 green chillies, deseeded and finely chopped
20g root ginger, peeled and finely grated
¾ teaspoon Kashmiri chilli powder
2 teaspoons chaat masala (see page 52)
3 tablespoons chopped coriander

NAANS

This yeasted bread is traditionally cooked in a hot tandoor – it's slapped onto the walls of the clay oven and left in place for less than a minute before being flicked out with a long metal rod. A domestic oven, set to its highest temperature, makes a good approximation of a tandoor. These naans, with their golden-speckled crust and soft, fluffy texture, are great for mopping up northern Indian classics, such as slow-cooked lentils with cream (see page 78) and paneer, peppers and spinach in makhani sauce (see page 107).

MAKES 8

500g strong white bread flour, plus extra for dusting
1 teaspoon salt
2 teaspoons caster sugar
2 teaspoons fast-action dried yeast
200g full-fat Greek yoghurt
50g ghee (see page 26) or unsalted butter, melted, plus extra for brushing
vegetable oil, for oiling

Sift the flour and salt into a bowl and whisk in the sugar and yeast. Make a well in the centre and pour in the yoghurt and melted ghee or butter. Add enough warm water to make a soft dough (the amount of water will depend on how absorbent the flour is, but it should be about 100ml).

Turn out the dough onto a floured surface and knead until smooth, then transfer it to a large, lightly oiled bowl. Turn over the dough so that the top is coated with a light film of oil. Cover with clingfilm and leave in a warm place for about 90 minutes, or until doubled in size.

Heat the oven to its hottest setting (about 240°C/220°C fan/gas mark 9) with 2 baking trays inside it. Punch down the dough, knead it again on a lightly oiled surface, then divide into 8 equal balls. Roll each ball into an oval-shaped naan, about 5mm thick. It's best to do this in batches of 4. Heat the grill to high.

Remove the hot baking trays from the oven and slap 2 naans onto each tray. Return the trays to the oven and cook for about 3 minutes, until the bread has puffed up.

Keep the naans on their baking trays and transfer each tray, one at a time, to the hot grill for about 30 seconds, or until the top of the breads browns. Brush with melted ghee or butter and serve straightaway or keep them warm wrapped in a clean tea towel or foil until ready to serve. Then, repeat the whole cooking process for the remaining dough balls.

PURIS

Puffed, deep-fried puris are especially popular across central India. In West Bengal, they are called *luchis* and are made with plain flour, which makes for a softer texture. Although puris are best enjoyed straight from the pan, they do make great picnic food when wrapped in foil and served with crushed tamarind potatoes (see page 63) or chickpea and potato curry (see page 77).

MAKES 12

Sift the flours and salt into a bowl. Work the oil into the flour with your fingers, then add enough cold water to make a firm dough. Knead until smooth (about 5 minutes), then shape it into a ball.

Put the dough in a lightly oiled bowl, cover, then leave to one side for at least 30 minutes for the dough to rest. Then, knead the dough and divide it equally into 12 balls, each about the size of a golf ball.

Slightly flatten the top of each ball and roll one out on an oiled surface to a 13cm-diameter circle, about 2.5mm thick. You can flip the dough over once or twice while you roll. Repeat the process with the remaining dough balls.

To deep-fry, fill a large, wide, sturdy pan no more than two-thirds full with oil. The oil is ready for frying when it reaches 180°C on a food thermometer, or when a cube of bread dropped into the oil browns in 30 seconds. Using a fish slice, lightly press on the top of the puri so that it puffs up as it cooks. After about 1 minute, flip the puri over and cook for a further 1 minute. Drain on kitchen paper and repeat the process with the remaining puris.

125g chapati flour (*chapati atta*) or wholemeal flour
125g plain flour
½ teaspoon fine salt
2 tablespoons sunflower oil, plus extra 500ml for oiling and deep-frying

Clockwise from left: Naans (see page 150); Chapatis (see page 148); Puris (see page 151)

THALIPEETH
MULTIGRAIN SESAME AND CHILLI FLATBREADS

A variety of grains, pulses and lentils are milled into flour and used extensively in bread-making across Rajasthan, Gujarat and Maharashtra. This flatbread, made with warming and astringent spices, fresh herbs and diced onion, are especially popular across western India and incorporate sweet and mildly flavoured sorghum (*jowar*) flour.

The sorghum is grown widely in southern Asia and in Africa and is available from Indian grocery shops. It blends well with other flours – I've used it here with chapati, gram (made from chickpeas) and rice flours. It's worth noting that rice flour is much finer in texture than granular ground rice, which is sold in most supermarkets. Look for rice flour in specialist or Asian grocery shops.

MAKES 10

150g wholemeal chapati
   flour (*chapati atta*), or
   75g wholemeal flour
   and 75g plain flour
75g sorghum (*jowar*) flour
75g rice flour
75g gram flour
1 teaspoon salt
2 teaspoons ground roasted
   coriander seeds
1 teaspoon garam masala
   (see page 51)
1 teaspoon ground roasted
   cumin seeds
3 tablespoons chopped
   coriander
½ teaspoon Kashmiri
   chilli powder
2 tablespoons sesame seeds
¼ teaspoon ground turmeric
3 teaspoons jaggery or light
   brown soft sugar
1 large red onion, diced
30g root ginger, peeled and
   finely grated
2 green chillies, deseeded
   and finely chopped
50–75g ghee, melted
   (see page 26) or 3–4
   tablespoons sunflower oil

Mix all the flours together in a bowl. Add the remaining ingredients apart from the ghee or oil and make a well in the centre. Pour enough cold water into the well to make a firm dough. Knead until smooth, then cover and leave to one side for 30 minutes.

Divide the dough into 10 evenly sized balls, each about the size of a small tangerine, and cover with a clean tea towel. Lightly grease one side of the outside of 2 medium, plastic freezer bags with a little ghee. Put a portion of dough on the ghee-covered side of one of the bags and cover with the other bag, ghee-side downwards.

Use your fingers to pat and smooth out the dough between the bags, until it resembles a flat disc measuring about 2.5mm thick and 10cm in diameter.

Heat a griddle pan or a sturdy frying pan over a medium heat and add 1 teaspoon of ghee or oil. Oil the palm of one hand. Peel off the top layer of plastic and turn the flattened disc onto your oiled palm. Carefully flip it onto the griddle or frying pan.

Drizzle a further 1–2 teaspoons of ghee or oil around the edges of the flatbread and cook until it is light brown – about 2–3 minutes. Turn the bread over with a fish slice and cook for a further 1–2 minutes to brown the other side.

Transfer the bread to a plate and keep warm while you cook the remaining breads. Spread each flatbread with a little more ghee or oil as it comes off the griddle. Serve hot with plain yoghurt and pickle.

CURRY LEAF AND CORIANDER OIL

This aromatic oil is made with fresh curry and coriander leaves and provides a burst of zesty flavour when added to southern Indian curries. It also works a treat in salad dressings and is good for drizzling over soups, sauces and boiled rice.

MAKES 100ML

75ml sunflower oil
75ml olive oil
about 30 fresh curry leaves
1 small bunch of coriander,
   chopped

Warm the sunflower oil and olive oil in a small pan over a very low heat and add the curry leaves. Don't let the oil get too hot otherwise the leaves will start to fry – 1 minute at a very low heat should be enough. Take the pan off the heat, leave the oil to cool, then stir in the chopped coriander.

Blend the oil, curry leaves and coriander in a liquidiser and then strain the mixture through a double thickness of muslin or kitchen paper into a clean bowl or jug. Allow the oil to drip through the filter naturally – don't try to hurry the process or the oil will become cloudy. Pour the flavoured oil into a small, dry jar. Store at room temperature – it will stay fresh for 5–7 days.

KACHUMBER
MIXED SALAD

This everyday side salad (known as *kachumber*) is colourful, crunchy and simply dressed in spiced lime juice, with plenty of fresh coriander.

SERVES 4–6

1 cucumber, halved lengthways, deseeded and diced
3 tomatoes, quartered, deseeded and diced
1 red onion, finely diced
juice of 2 limes
¾ teaspoon ground roasted cumin seeds
1 red chilli, deseeded and finely chopped
½ teaspoon coarsely ground black peppercorns
2 teaspoons caster sugar
3 tablespoons chopped coriander

Combine the diced cucumber, tomato and onion in a bowl.

In a separate bowl, mix the lime juice with the ground cumin, red chilli, black pepper, sugar and chopped coriander to make a dressing, then pour this over the salad. Stir well and then leave the salad to one side for 15 minutes, so that the flavours mingle.

PICKLED MOOLI, RADISH AND FENNEL

This mild and crisp-textured pickle takes on a lovely pink hue from the red radishes as they steep in the sweetly spiced, vinegary liquor.

MAKES 500G

Top and tail the red radishes, then shave them on a mandolin or thinly slice with a sharp knife. Shave the white radish and fennel in the same way and then mix the vegetables together in a bowl with the sliced ginger and lime juice.

To make the pickling liquor, pour 150ml of water into a pan and add all the pickling ingredients. Place over a low heat until the sugar dissolves, then increase the heat to medium and cook for 5 minutes. Pour the hot liquor over the vegetables and leave to cool.

Spoon the vegetables into a sterilised jar and cover with the spiced liquor (a 750ml jar works well, so that the liquor completely covers the vegetables). Leave to mature for 2–3 days before using. The pickle will keep in the fridge for 3–4 months.

1 small bunch of red radish
(about 8–10), leaves removed
150g white radish
(*mooli*), peeled
1 small bulb of fennel
20g root ginger, peeled and
sliced into thin matchsticks
juice of 1 lime

FOR THE PICKLING LIQUOR
100ml white wine vinegar
50g caster sugar
1 teaspoon salt
1 teaspoon fennel seeds
½ teaspoon dried red chilli flakes

TAMARIND PULP
TECHNIQUE

The fruit from the pods of a tamarind tree have a pleasing sourness and the strained pulp provides a tart, fruity flavour to masalas, sauces and chutneys. Tamarind is normally sold in dried blocks or semi-dried ones (known as wet tamarind), and is also available as a concentrate.

MAKES 6–8 TABLESPOONS

200g wet, seedless tamarind block

Break up the tamarind block with your hands and put it in a heatproof bowl. Pour over enough boiling water to cover generously and soak for 15–20 minutes, until it is totally soft. Leave to one side to cool.

Push the tamarind pulp through a metal sieve and discard any fibres. Sometimes a fine-meshed sieve can become clogged with the pulp. It's best to use a coarse sieve, conical strainer or even a colander instead. Add a little water if the tamarind is too thick to easily pass through the sieve. Aim for a consistency similar to a cake batter.

FIVE TIPS WHEN BUYING AND USING TAMARIND

- If you can find it, buy wet, seedless tamarind blocks, which are available from most southern Indian and Southeast Asian shops.

- Many northern Indian shops sell dried blocks of tamarind, which have seeds – they will take longer to soften and involve a lot more effort when pushing the pulp through a sieve. However, it's a viable alternative if wet tamarind blocks are unavailable.

- Tamarind has a long shelf life and keeps for about 1 year at room temperature. Store opened packets in an airtight bag.

- Using a tamarind concentrate may be convenient, but it has a metallic aftertaste and doesn't match the quality of pulp made at home.

- Make a big batch of tamarind pulp, then spoon small quantities into ice-cube trays and freeze until solid. Once set, transfer the cubes to a bag and store them in the freezer. The cubes will keep for 6–8 months, or more.

NINE DISHES THAT USE TAMARIND PULP

- Chaat masala fruit salad (see page 38)

- Tamarind and vegetable lentils (see page 81)

- Date and tamarind sauce (see page 167)

- Crushed tamarind potatoes (see page 63)

- Gujarati sweet-and-sour dal (see page 71)

- South Indian rice and lentil pulao (see page 138)

- Aubergines with peanut masala (see page 102)

- Kohlrabi broth (see page 127)

- Green chilli pickle (see page 160)

GREEN CHILLI PICKLE

This is a simple, southern Indian chilli pickle, emboldened by garlicky tamarind and curry leaf masala, and enriched with pounded peanuts and coconut.

MAKES 300G

75ml sunflower oil
about 30 fresh curry leaves
1 large onion, diced
1 garlic bulb, cloves separated,
    peeled and finely chopped
30g root ginger, peeled and
    finely chopped
30ml white wine vinegar
½ teaspoon ground turmeric
150g fat, green Turkish chillies
    (about 4 or 5), slit, deseeded
    and cut into 1cm pieces
3 tablespoons wet tamarind pulp,
    seedless (see page 158)

FOR THE SEASONING

1 tablespoon unsalted
    peanuts, skinned
2 tablespoons desiccated
    coconut
1 tablespoon coriander seeds
2 teaspoons cumin seeds
1 tablespoon sesame seeds

Heat the oil in a karahi or wok over a medium heat. Add the curry leaves and fry them for a few seconds, until aromatic. Add the onion and continue frying for 8–10 minutes, until golden. Stir in the garlic and ginger and cook for a further 1 minute, until the garlic and ginger have cooked out.

Add the vinegar and turmeric and simmer for about 2 minutes, until the vinegar has evaporated. Stir in the chopped green chillies and cook over a low heat for 3–5 minutes, stirring occasionally, and then set aside.

To make the seasoning, heat a sturdy frying pan over a medium heat and add the peanuts. Roast them, stirring all the time, for 2–3 minutes, until they pick up flecks of colour. Add the coconut, followed by the coriander, cumin and sesame seeds, and roast for a further 2–3 minutes, until the spices are fragrant. Cool the spice mix, then transfer to an electric grinder and process to a coarse powder. (You could pound it with a mortar and pestle if you don't have a grinder.)

Mix the seasoning with the green chilli mixture in the pan. Place over a medium heat and cook, uncovered, for 2 minutes, then stir in the tamarind pulp. Take the pan off the heat and leave the pickle to cool before spooning into a sterilised jar. It will keep for at least 3–4 months at room temperature.

CARROT CHUTNEY

Simmer carrots down with ginger and garlic in chilli-vinegar syrup and you'll create translucent shreds infused with the warmth of garam masala, cumin and sesame seeds.

MAKES 700G

Put the carrots in a colander, generously sprinkle with the salt and set aside for 1 hour. Using your hands, squeeze any excess water from the carrots.

Put the sugar and vinegar in a medium pan over a low heat. Allow the sugar to dissolve (about 2–3 minutes), stirring occasionally. Add the squeezed, grated carrots, along with the ginger, garlic, chilli powder, cumin and garam masala, and stir to combine.

Cook the spiced carrots over a medium heat for about 30 minutes, until most of the liquid has evaporated, then stir in the raisins and sesame seeds and continue cooking until the carrot shreds are glossy and dry.

Leave the chutney to cool, then spoon it into a sterilised jar and seal. This chutney is best left to mature for 2 days before using and will keep for 2–3 months in a cool, dry place.

500g carrots, peeled and
    coarsely grated
1 teaspoon salt, for sprinkling
250g caster sugar
350ml white wine vinegar
20g root ginger, peeled and
    finely grated
4 garlic cloves, finely chopped
½ teaspoon Kashmiri
    chilli powder
½ teaspoon ground roasted
    cumin seeds
½ teaspoon garam masala
    (see page 51)
50g raisins
2 tablespoons roasted
    sesame seeds

BENGALI TOMATO CHUTNEY

A Bengali spice mix, *panch phoron* (see page 54), gives this sweet-and-sour chutney its characteristically pickled flavour. Serve it warm or at room temperature with baby spinach pakoras (see page 15) and other fried snacks.

MAKES 600G

3 tablespoons sunflower oil
1 teaspoon *panch phoron*
   (see page 54)
1 red onion, diced
4 garlic cloves, finely chopped
25g root ginger, peeled and
   finely chopped
½ teaspoon dried red chilli flakes
1 green chilli, deseeded and
   finely chopped
1 x 400g can of chopped
   tomatoes
75g pitted dates, chopped
25g caster sugar, plus extra to
   taste if needed
25ml white wine vinegar

Heat the oil in a medium pan over a medium heat, then fry the *panch phoron* for a few seconds, until the seeds are fragrant. Reduce the heat to low and add the remaining ingredients. Pour over 100ml of water and simmer, uncovered, for 10–15 minutes, until thickened to a slack paste-like consistency. The chutney should have a sweet-and-sour flavour – add a little more sugar, if needed. Transfer to a sterilised jar and enjoy at its best within 2–3 days.

FRESH CORIANDER CHUTNEY

This refreshing relish features an abundance of coriander, its citrussy flavour working well with the punchy notes of garlic, ginger and chilli.

MAKES 250G

Blend all the ingredients except the cashew nuts in a liquidiser with a splash of hot water. Once the mixture is smooth, drain the nuts from their soaking liquid and add them to the liquidiser and process again. Aim for a sweet and tangy flavour – you may need to add more sugar or lime juice to get the balance right. Transfer the chutney to a bowl and cover. Store it in the fridge and use it on the same day.

large handful of coriander, roughly chopped
2 tablespoons chopped mint leaves
1 small green pepper, deseeded and roughly chopped
2–3 teaspoons caster sugar, plus extra to taste if needed
1 teaspoon ground roasted cumin seeds
20g root ginger, peeled and roughly chopped
2 large garlic cloves, roughly chopped
1 green chilli, roughly chopped
juice of ½ lime, plus extra to taste
25g cashew nuts, soaked in hot water for 30 minutes

RED CHILLI AND GARLIC CHUTNEY

This lively chutney is made with mild Kashmiri chillies spiked with fried ginger, garlic and tomatoes. It's great served with savoury snacks, such as samosas (see page 37), or as a condiment for main meals.

MAKES 250G

10 dried Kashmiri chillies
3 tablespoons sunflower oil
25g root ginger, peeled and
    finely grated
8 garlic cloves, finely chopped
1 x 400g can of chopped
    tomatoes
3 teaspoons caster sugar
1 teaspoon ground roasted
    cumin seeds
1 teaspoon ground roasted
    coriander seeds
juice of 1 lime

Using scissors, snip the tops off the dried chillies and shake out and discard most of the seeds (the seeds are quite stubborn, so just do your best). Soak the chillies in hot water for 20 minutes to rehydrate, then drain them, reserving the soaking water.

While the chillies are soaking, heat the oil in a small pan over a medium heat. Add the ginger and garlic and fry for 1–2 minutes, until fragrant. Add the tomatoes and sugar and cook for 10–15 minutes, until the chutney has darkened and reduced to a paste-like consistency.

Grind the rehydrated chillies to a coarse paste in a small food processor, adding a ladleful of the soaking liquid to help it on its way. Then, stir the ground cumin and coriander into the chutney, followed by the ground chilli paste. Continue cooking for 2–3 minutes to cook out the spices, then take the pan off the heat and add enough lime juice to sharpen.

Leave the chutney to cool, then spoon it into a sterilised jar. Store it in the fridge, where it will keep for about 1 week.

SHREDDED MANGO CHUTNEY

For the best results, choose unripe green mangoes bought from Asian stores – their sourness counters the sweetness of gingery syrup and complements the astringency of ginger and nigella seeds.

MAKES 400G

Mix the grated mango with the chilli powder, turmeric, black pepper, ground cumin and salt, and set aside for 1 hour.

When the mango is ready, heat the oil in a karahi or wok over a medium heat. Add the nigella and fennel seeds and fry for about 30 seconds, until the fennel is aromatic.

Stir in the ginger, followed by the grated mango and 125ml of water. Bring the chutney to the boil, then add the vinegar and sugar. Reduce the heat and allow the sugar to dissolve, stirring occasionally, and then increase the heat again and boil the chutney for about 10 minutes, until the fruit softens and the syrup thickens.

Take the pan off the heat and leave to cool before transferring the chutney to a sterilised jar. Store at room temperature for up to 6 months.

500g unripe green
    mangoes, peeled, stoned
    and coarsely grated
½ teaspoon Kashmiri
    chilli powder
¼ teaspoon ground turmeric
¼ teaspoon coarsely ground
    black peppercorns
½ teaspoon ground roasted
    cumin seeds
1 teaspoon salt
3 tablespoons sunflower oil
¼ teaspoon nigella seeds
1 teaspoon fennel seeds
30g root ginger, peeled and
    finely grated
3 tablespoons white wine vinegar
450g caster sugar

RAITAS

Cooling and refreshing raitas are made from spiced yoghurt and fruit or vegetables. They refresh the palate, provide a light contrast to rich masalas and are especially welcome when served with a heavy meal.

SERVES 4

CUCUMBER RAITA

1 small cucumber, cut
    lengthways, deseeded and
    coarsely grated
300g full-fat Greek yoghurt
½ teaspoon ground roasted
    cumin seeds
1 garlic clove, crushed
1 teaspoon caster sugar
1 small shallot, finely diced
1 tablespoon finely chopped
    mint leaves

Using your hands, squeeze any juice from the grated cucumber. Put it in a mixing bowl and combine with the remaining ingredients.

BEETROOT RAITA

1 small raw beetroot, peeled and
    coarsely grated
300g full-fat Greek yoghurt
1 small red onion, finely diced
½ teaspoon ground roasted
    cumin seeds
1 green chilli, deseeded and
    finely chopped
1 tablespoon chopped dill

Put the grated beetroot in a mixing bowl and combine with the remaining ingredients.

POMEGRANATE RAITA

75g pomegranate seeds
300g full-fat Greek yoghurt
½ teaspoon chaat masala
    (see page 52)
½ teaspoon ground roasted
    cumin seeds
¼ teaspoon Kashmiri chilli powder
1 teaspoon caster sugar
1 tablespoon chopped coriander

Reserve 1 tablespoon of the pomegranate seeds. Place the remainder in a mixing bowl and mix with the other ingredients. Transfer the mixture to a serving bowl and scatter with the reserved pomegranate seeds.

DATE AND TAMARIND SAUCE

This sweet and tangy sauce (known as *sonth*) comes from Gujarat in western India. It's a great match with creamy yoghurt and is often drizzled over salads and served with samosas and pakoras.

MAKES 300G

Break up the tamarind and dates and put them in a pan with the jaggery or sugar and enough water to cover – about 500ml. Place over a medium-low heat and bring the chutney to a simmer. Cook for about 20–30 minutes, adding extra water to the pan if the chutney looks like catching, until the tamarind and dates are really soft and pulpy.

Remove the pan from the heat and push the sauce through a sieve to remove any fibres.

Stir in the ginger, garam masala and cumin. Taste the sauce – it should have a sweet-and-sour flavour. Add more jaggery or sugar if it isn't sweet enough. Serve chilled. It will keep for 2–3 days in the fridge, or 2 months in the freezer.

150g wet tamarind block
125g pitted dates
175g jaggery or light brown soft sugar, plus extra to taste if needed
1 teaspoon ground ginger
½ teaspoon garam masala (see page 51)
1 teaspoon ground roasted cumin seeds

INDEX

A

Adrak Phool Gobi 64
almonds and saffron sauce 112
Ande Bhujia 30
aubergine
  in garlicky tomato masala 135
  with peanut masala 102
  smoky mash 60

B

Baby Spinach Pakoras 15
Baghare Baingan 102
Baingan Bharta 60
basmati rice 136
  jackfruit and orange
    biryani 92
  see also puffed rice; pulaos
beans 72
  butterbean and cashew
    masala 74
  kidney beans with tomatoes
    and ginger 86
beetroot
  with curry leaves and
    coconut 45
  raita 166
Bengali Tomato Chutney 162
Bhel Puri 33
Bhutta Ka Kees 145
bread
  chapatis 148
  chilli cheese toast 34
  multigrain sesame and chilli
    flatbread 154
  naans 150
  puris 151
  white radish parathas 149
Bulgur Wheat and Cardamom
  Tikkis 20
butter
  smoked cardamom 29
  see also ghee
Butterbean and Cashew
  Masala 74

butternut squash
  and sweet potato
    vindaloo 118
  tandoori with red onion
    raita 123

C

caramel and orange sauce 20
cardamom
  and bulgur wheat tikkis 20
  and chilli potatoes 49
  smoked butter 29
carrots
  chutney 161
  and lentil and coconut
    pachadi 68
cashew nuts
  and butterbean masala 74
  sauce 132
cauliflower
  with ginger 64
  in saffron and almond
    sauce 112
Chaat Masala 52
Chaat Masala Fruit Salad 38
Chana Alu Masala 77
Channa chaat 12
Chapatis 148
charcoal 120
cheese
  chilli toast 34
  see also paneer
chickpeas
  and potato curry 77
  salad 12
Chilli Cheese Toast 34
chillies *see* dried chilli; green
  chilli; red chilli
chutneys
  carrot 161
  coconut 124
  coriander 163
  mango 165
  red chilli and garlic 164
  tomato 162
  see also relishes
coconut
  carrot and lentil pachadi 68

chutney 124
  and beetroot with curry
    leaves 45
  and pea pancakes 16
coriander
  chutney 163
  and curry leaf oil 155
cream
  Rajasthani onions 59
  slow-cooked lentils 78
  and spinach sauce 141
Crisp-Fried Okra with Mango
  Relish 23
Crispy Cauliflower in Saffron and
  Almond Sauce 112
Crushed Tamarind Potatoes 63
cucumber raita 166
cumin red peppers in tomato
  masala 56
curries
  aubergines in garlicky tomato
    masala 135
  butterbean and cashew 74
  chickpea and potato 77
  egg 138
  ginger-spiced pineapple and
    tomato 101
  kohlrabi broth 127
  southern-style mango 98
  squash and sweet potato
    vindaloo 118
  sweetcorn 145
  vegetable korma 115
curry leaves
  and beetroot with coconut 45
  and coriander oil 155

D

dals
  green gram 89
  Gujarati sweet-and-sour 71
  lime 82
  slow-cooked with cream 78
  tarka 85
Date and Tamarind Sauce 167
doughnuts ginger and green
  chilli 24

ACKNOWLEDGEMENTS

Huge gratitude to the publishing team at Absolute – there would be no book without their expertise. My great appreciation to Jon Croft for making that first phone call; Meg Boas for commissioning me; Emily North for her unrivalled editing skills and unstinting support and Marie O'Shepherd for eye-catching design layouts and artwork. Thanks also to assistant designer, Anika Schulze, copy editor Judy Barratt, proofreader Margaret Haynes and Elaine Byfield for road-testing recipes ahead of the photo shoot.

The wonderful David Loftus elevated dishes to star status with his outstanding photography. And fellow author and home economist, Rukmini Iyer and her team of Jo Jackson and Alex Dorgan, seamlessly co-ordinated kitchen activity while braving London's Indian summer heatwave. Respect!

I'm indebted to the late Ronnie Lobo, formerly general manager at Delhi's Taj Mahal Hotel, and his chefs. Some of the dishes in this book have been inspired by my time there during the 1990s. I'd also like to thank my old friend Karunesh Khanna, head chef at Tamarind restaurant – a version of his fig and spinach tikkis appears in this book.

To my dear friend Diana Henry, and fellow members of The Guild of Food Writers, especially Angela Clutton, Sam Kilgour, Jenny Linford and Jonathan Woods. Nothing beats a large G&T and rock solid support in keeping the motor running.

For Ruth Cowen and Geeta Dhingra, thank you for believing in me and not balking when I cut short our conversations to hack at a jackfruit. And I salute you for putting up with my meltdown when the local Indian shop ran out of Kashmiri chillies. Denise Wallin and Yesim Douwana, what would I have done without your laughter after I confided that I was in love with my pressure cooker? There's a Tupperware box crammed with samosas waiting for you.

Both my daughters, Malvika and Pallavi, made space in their fridges and freezers for close to 100 foil boxes while recipe testing was in full flow. Even my 15-month-old granddaughter joined the Gulati culinary team and catapulted rice and lentil pulao over her hair, gamely landing a few grains on target.

Finally, to Dan, my wonderful husband, thank you for the late night editing sessions, the cups of tea, stiff drinks and snacks. There's nothing like the crunch of cheese and onion crisps at midnight to keep me motivated for an impending deadline. For a man accustomed to reading serious fiction, having to check the accuracy of ingredients for mattar paneer, must have been a novel, but no less moving, experience.

Finally to my late mum – every evening, she tucked her sari around her and, with gold bangles jangling, set about making a full-on Punjabi supper. I regret never getting to thank her for those meals and for our shared cooking sessions in the 1970s. I'm setting the record straight now.

Publisher
Jon Croft

Commissioning Editor
Meg Boas

Senior Editor
Emily North

Art Director & Design
Marie O'Shepherd

Junior Designer & Cover Design
Anika Schulze

Photography
David Loftus

Food Styling
Rukmini Iyer

Food Styling Assistants
Jo Jackson
Alex Dorgan

Home Economy
Elaine Byfield

Copyeditor
Judy Barratt

Proofreader
Margaret Haynes

Indexer
Zoe Ross

BLOOMSBURY ABSOLUTE

Bloomsbury Publishing Plc
50 Bedford Square, London, WC1B 3DP, UK

BLOOMSBURY, BLOOMSBURY ABSOLUTE, the Diana logo and the Absolute Press logo are trademarks of Bloomsbury Publishing Plc.

First published in Great Britain, 2020

A catalogue record for this book is available from the British Library.

Library of Congress Cataloguing-in-Publication data has been applied for.

ISBN: 9781472971968
ePUB: 9781472971975
ePDF: 9781472971982

2 4 6 8 10 9 7 5 3 1

Printed and bound in China by Toppan Leefung Printing.

Bloomsbury Publishing Plc makes every effort to ensure that the papers used in the manufacture of our books are natural, recyclable products made from wood grown in well-managed forests. Our manufacturing processes conform to the environmental regulations of the country of origin.

To find out more about our authors and books visit www.bloomsbury.com and sign up for our newsletters.